Living Language®
English for New Americans

Everyday Life

Also available from Living Language:

Educational discounts for **English for New Americans** are available.
To order or inquire, please call 1-800-733-3000.

Living Language®
English for New Americans

Everyday Life

Written by

Carol Piñeiro, Ed.D.
Boston University

Edited by

Ana Stojanović, M.A.

Living Language, A Random House Company
New York

Living Language books and packages are available at special discounts for bulk purchases for premiums and sales promotions, as well as for fund-raising or educational use. For more information, contact the Special Sales Manager at the address below.

Published by Living Language, A Random House Company,
201 East 50th Street, New York, New York 10022

Random House, Inc. New York, Toronto, London, Sydney, Auckland

www.livinglanguage.com

Living Language is a registered trademark of Random House, Inc.

Printed in the United States of America

Cover and package design by David Tran

Interior design by Alexander Taylor

Illustrations by Christopher Medellín and Josef Medellín

Library of Congress Cataloging-in-Publication-Data is available upon request.

ISBN 0-609-80620-3

10 9 8 7 6 5 4 3 2 1

First Edition

To my daughter, Aliana Houser Piñeiro, whose love and humor have helped me through this project.

Acknowledgements

Many thanks to the Living Language staff: Lisa Alpert, Christopher Warnasch, Christopher Medellín, Eric Sommer, Germaine Ma, Helen Tang, Andrea Rosen, David Tran, and Liana Parry Faughnan. Special thanks to the staff of VPG: Al Browne, Doug Latham, Raquel Ortiz, Sabrina Aviles, Andrei Campeanu, and Alex Taylor.

Contents

Living Language®
English for New Americans

Everyday Life

Introduction

Welcome to *English for New Americans,* a series of language learning programs from Living Language. *English for New Americans* will greatly improve your ability to speak and understand "real" American English. The complete course consists of this workbook, one 60-minute videocassette, one 60-minute audio-cassette, and an audioscript.

The *English for New Americans* program uses an immersion approach, so you'll be using English from the start, just as you would in real life. The program provides you with the tools you'll need—vocabulary, phrases, and basic grammar—to help you communicate in typical situations in the United States. We recommend that you also buy a good dictionary for reference.

How to Use the Program

The *English for New Americans* 1-2-3 method makes the program very easy to use.

I. WATCH A UNIT ON THE VIDEO.
Put the video cassette into your VCR, sit back, and watch a unit straight through on the video. Don't worry if you don't understand everything the first time around. You'll have the chance to watch again. Pay attention to facial expressions, body language and the surroundings as you watch. You might be surprised at just how much you already understand! After the first viewing, you may want to write down a brief summary of what you think happened in the *Watch and Listen* section. When you're done, rewind to the beginning of the unit.

2. WATCH AGAIN. READ AND WRITE IN THE WORKBOOK.
Watch the same unit again. When you see the ▶️ symbol on screen, stop the tape and go to the workbook. Complete the exercises in order until you reach the 📼 symbol. Then continue watching the video again until you reach the next ▶️ symbol. In each unit, you will be asked to complete exercises following the *See it, Hear it, Say it* section, following the *Watch and Listen* section, and again following the *Real People...Real Language* section. Remember: whenever you see this: ▶️ , go to the workbook; when you see the 📼 symbol in the workbook, go back to the video.

After you've completed all the exercises in the workbook, watch the video unit one more time. Compare how much you are able to understand this time with the first viewing! Look at the summary you wrote—how much were you able to understand? As the program continues, you'll find that you're making real progress.

3. LISTEN AND SPEAK.
Once you've studied with the video and completed the exercises in the workbook, you can practice what you've learned using the audio cassette. Just put it into your cassette player, and listen and repeat wherever it's convenient—at home, on your way to work, while doing housework, or whenever you have a spare ten minutes.

Focus on the sounds of the language. Don't worry if your accent isn't perfect. The more you practice, the more it will improve. In the United States, people speak with a wide variety of accents, but everyone is still able to communicate. As you will see on the video, Jorge, Elena, Ming, and Sasha all have foreign accents, but they are able to get their messages across, and that's what counts!

Materials

• ONE 60-MINUTE VIDEO CASSETTE
In the *English for New Americans* video series, you'll meet Simon and Raquel, a couple who volunteers at an International Center, assisting and advising new immigrants as they adjust to life in the United States. You will also get to know Jorge and Elena, a married couple from Mexico; Sasha, a Russian house-painter; and Ming, a waitress from Hong Kong with ambitions of opening her own restaurant. Why don't you join them? Simon and Raquel will be *your* guides as well as theirs.

The video comprises seven units, each dealing with a practical situation. Each unit consists of three sections:

See it, hear it, say it
In this section you will learn key vocabulary relating to the topic of the unit. You will hear how to pronounce the word, see what it means, and see how it's spelled in English. Repeat each new word that you learn.

Watch and Listen
This section is the heart of each unit. You'll see and hear language relating to the topic of the unit. At the end of the section, you'll hear a brief review of a few important phrases.

Real People...Real Language
This section features interviews with real people who will tell you about their lives in the United States. This is your chance to hear and practice real language.

Each section in the unit builds on the preceding one, and the language becomes more challenging, so you'll see progress in every unit! What's more, you'll hear English as it's really spoken, so you'll be able to understand regional or foreign accents and use what you learn in daily life.

• 144-PAGE WORKBOOK

In the workbook, you'll find exercises to help you build your vocabulary and learn the basic rules of English and how to apply them. You'll also see brief explanations of key concepts. You might be asked to do some of the following:

☞ name an object or person you saw on the video
☞ fill in the correct form of a verb
☞ answer questions with "yes" or "no"
☞ choose the correct answer from several options
☞ match the beginning of a sentence with an ending, or match a question with its answer
☞ fill in missing information

The first one or two questions in each exercise are completed for you, showing you what to do. You can find all the answers at the back of the book in the Answer Key.

At the end of each unit in the workbook, you'll find a complete transcript of the *Watch and Listen* segments from the video. In addition, you can find all of the words used in the program in the word list at the back of the book.

• ONE 60-MINUTE AUDIO CASSETTE

Once you've watched the video and completed the exercises in the workbook, you can use the audio cassette to review and practice what you learned in each unit. Each unit on the audio cassette consists of three sections: first you will review key vocabulary and phrases that were used on the video and in the workbook. Just listen and repeat after the native speakers in the pauses provided. Next, you'll hear an excerpt from the scene you saw on the video, and again you'll have a chance to repeat the phrases yourself. Finally, you'll be asked to respond to questions and make sentences on your own. Again, the language you use will build from one section to the next, until, by the end, you'll be speaking on your own!

• AUDIO SCRIPT

The pocket-size audio script contains a complete transcript of everything you'll hear on the audio cassette. You can look up words you didn't understand or see how the phrases are written.

Now, let's get started…

Introducción

Bienvenidos a *English for New Americans*, una serie de programas de aprendizaje de Living Language que le ayudar a dominar y hablar el inglés como en realidad se habla en los Estados Unidos. El curso completo consiste de este cuaderno, un video y un audiocassette de 60 minutos, y ademas el libreto del audiocassette.

El programa *English for New Americans* tiene un enfoque de inmersión para que usted hable inglés desde el principio, tal y como se hace en la vida real. El programa le proporcionar los instrumentos necesarios—desde el vocabulario, las frases y los enunciados hasta la gramática—para que usted pueda comunicarse de la manera más normal y típica en los Estados Unidos. Es importante tener un excelente diccionario, le ayudar muchisimo.

Cómo usar el programa

El método 1-2-3 de *English for New Americans* hace que este curso sea fácil de entender y todavía más fácil de usar.

1. VEA UNA UNIDAD DEL VIDEO.

Meta el videocassette en su videocasetera, póngase cómodo, y vea una unidad completa. No se preocupe si no entiende toda la unidad la primera vez que la vea. Tendrá la oportunidad de verla las veces que desee. Preste atención y fíjese en los gestos de los personajes, sus expresiones, la manera cómo mueven su cuerpo y lo que esté sucediendo a su alrededor. ¡Quedar sorprendido al darse cuenta de todo lo que entiende al solamente ver lo que acontece en el video! Después de ver la sección titulada *Watch and Listen* (Vea y Escuche) una vez, escriba un breve resumen de lo que usted acaba de ver en esta sección. Si no la captó en su totalidad, escriba sobre lo que sí entendió. Al terminar, recorra el video hasta el principio de esta misma unidad.

2. VÉALA OTRA VEZ. LEA Y ESCRIBA EN SU CUADERNO.

Vuelva a ver la primera unidad. Cuando vea este símbolo ▶🗐 en la pantalla, detenga el video y abra el cuaderno. Haga los ejercicios indicados hasta llegar a este otro símbolo: 📼. Esto significa que debe dejar de escribir y regresar al video una vez más. Esto sucederá con cada unidad: verá el video una vez, lo verá por segunda vez, hará ejercicios, y regresará al video. Este proceso se repitirá después de haber visto la sección titulada *See it, Hear it, Say it* (Véalo, Escúchelo, Repítalo), después de ver la sección *Watch and Listen* (Vea y Escuche), y también después de ver la sección *Real People...Real Language* (La Gente y el Idioma Real). Recuerde: cuando vea este símbolo ▶🗐 usted tendrá que dejar de ver el video y empezar a trabajar en el cuaderno; y cuando vea este otro símbolo 📼 cierre su cuaderno y póngase a ver el video nuevamente.

Después de haber terminado todos los ejercicios que se encuentran en este cuaderno, vea el video una vez más. ¿Se acuerda cuanto pudo captar la primera vez que vió esta unidad? ¿Cuánto entendio esta última vez? ¡Lea el resumen que escribió sobre la primera unidad y se dará cuenta que va progresando poco a poco y que ahora entiende mucho más!

3. ESCUCHE Y REPITA.

Después de haber estudiado con el video y el cuaderno, puede practicar lo que ha aprendido usando el audiocassette. Escúchelo y repita todo lo que oiga. Esto lo puede hacer cuando desee: en casa, en camino al trabajo, al hacer los quehaceres del hogar, en fin, cuando usted pueda o tenga unos 10 o 15 minutos libres.

Concéntrese en los sonidos del idioma. No se preocupe si su acento no es perfecto. Entre más practique, mejor hablará y pronunciará el inglés. Todo es cuestión de dedicarle tiempo y esfuerzo a este programa. Ahora, recuerde que en los Estados Unidos hay inmigrantes de todos los países y con todos los acentos del mundo, sin embargo, logran entender y comunicarse. Como verá en el video, Jorge, Elena, Ming, y Sasha tienen acentos extranjeros, sin embargo, logran convivir y entenderse entre si mismos y, pues, ¿qué no es lo que más importa?

Materiales
• UN VIDEOCASSETTE DE 60 MINUTOS

En esta serie de videos *English for New Americans*, usted conocerá a Simon y Raquel. Ellos son una pareja que trabaja en el Centro Internacional ayudando y aconsejando a gente que acaba de llegar a los Estados Unidos, individuos como usted que se están adaptando a este país y a sus costumbres. También conocerá a Jorge y Elena, una pareja recién llegada de México; Sasha, un pintor de casas, ruso y a Ming, una mesera china con ilusiones de abrir su propio restaurante. Simon y Raquel los guiarán para ayudarles a evitar muchos de los problemas que todos enfrentamos al llegar por primera vez a este país sin hablar el idioma.

El video consiste de siete unidades, cada una trata con un problema o situación de la vida cotidiana. Cada unidad está compuesta de tres secciones:

See it, Hear it, Say it (Escúchelo, Véalo, y Dígalo)
En esta sección le daremos a conocer el vocabulario relacionado con el tema de la unidad. Usted escuchará cómo se pronuncia cada palabra, verá lo que significa y también cómo se escribe en inglés. Trate de repetir cada palabra que vaya viendo. Recuerde, si no lo puede hacer la primera vez, tendrá la oportunidad de volverlo a intentar las veces que desee.

Watch and Listen (Vea y Escuche)
Esta es la sección más importante de cada unidad. Usted verá y escuchará el idioma y lenguaje relacionado con cada unidad. Al terminar cada sección, escuchará un breve repaso de las frases y expresiones más importantes.

Real People-Real Language (La Gente y el Idioma Real)
En esta sección figuran entrevistas con personas que hablarán sobre sus vidas en los Estados Unidos. Estas entrevistas le brindarán la oportunidad de escuchar y practicar el inglés cotidiano, el inglés estadounidense. Cada sección está basada en la anterior, así es cómo usted irá progresando poco a poco. No solo eso, sino que usted escuchará y aprenderá inglés cómo en realidad se habla, y no el inglés británico o formal. De esta manera podrá identificar los diferentes acentos

regionales y extranjeros y podrá usar todo lo que ha aprendido ante situaciones de la vida diaria.

• UN CUADERNO DE 144 PÁGINAS

El cuaderno contiene los ejercicios que le ayudarán a ampliar su vocabulario y aprender las reglas básicas del inglés junto con su aplicación. También verá explicaciones básicas de conceptos clave, es decir, los conceptos del idioma de más importancia. En los ejercicios le pediremos que:

☞ nombre personas u objetos que haya visto en el video
☞ escriba o conplete el verbo en forma correcta
☞ conteste preguntas con respuestas sencillas yes/si o no
☞ escoja la respuesta correcta, de entre varias opciones
☞ relacione adecuadamente el comienzo de un enunciado con su terminación
☞ relacione correctamente una pregunta con su respuesta
☞ responda adecuadamente a preguntas en forma escrita

Las primeras preguntas siempre incluirán la respuesta y le servirán como ejemplo o modelo. Conteste el resto de los ejercicios siguiendo estos ejemplos. El resto de las respuestas las encontrará en la sección posterior del cuaderno titulada, Answer Key (Clave de Respuestas).

Al final de cada unidad del cuaderno encontrará la transcripción de todo lo que vió y escuchó en el video. ¡También encontrará en la sección posterior del libro una lista de todas las palabras que se han usado y que ha escuchado en el video y el cassette!

• EL AUDIOCASSETTE

Ya que haya visto la unidad en el video y terminado los ejercicios en el cuaderno, usted podrá repasar y practicar lo que aprendió usando el audiocassette. Sólo tiene que escuchar y repetir lo que se dice en la cinta. Toque su audiocassette y escuchará a personas hablando inglés y repasando las frases y el vocabulario que usted ya escuchó y vio en su video y cuaderno. También tendrá la oportunidad de hacer y contestar preguntas, crear sus propias oraciones, y cambiar oraciones sustituyendo una palabra por otra. Primero, escuche el ejemplo dado en el audiocassette y conteste con la respuesta adecuada. Después de una pequeña pausa, escuchará la respuesta correcta. ¡El audiocassette también es ideal para practicar la pronunciación y eliminar el acento!

• EL GUIÓN DEL ADIOCASSETTE

El guión del audiocassette es un libreto de bolsillo que contiene una transcripción completa de todo lo que se escucha en el audiocassette. En este pequeño libreto podrá ver cómo se escriben ciertas palabras, podrá buscar las palabras o frases que no llegó a captar, o simplemente le servirá ya sea como fuente de información o como guía de estudio.

Ahora, comencemos...

引言

欢迎使用Living Language® 编辑出版的 "新移民英语" 系列课程。"新移民英语" 将大大加强你对 "真正" 的美式英语的理解能力，并提高你的会话水平。整套课程包括练习手册，一盘六十分钟的录影带，一盘六十分钟的录音带和录音原稿。

"新移民英语" 使用浸透式教学方法，让你一开始就使用英语进行交谈，就象在真实生活中一样。本课程为你提供交流所必需的工具--词汇，短语及基本语法--协助你在美国实际生活中进行交流。我们建议你同时购买一本好的字典，参照使用。

使用方法

"新移民英语" 使用的三步法非常容易。

一、先看一段录影带

把录影带放入录影机，坐下来欣赏一个单元的录像。即使第一遍没有完全看懂也不用着急，因为你回头可以重复再看。应多注意人物的面部表情和肢体语言及周围景物。你或许会感到惊奇的是实际上你已经懂得不少了！看过一遍以后，你可以把你在看听时段的情景写一个简单的小结。此后，再把录影带倒回到这一单元的起点。

二、重看录影带，然后作练习手册中的读写练习

重看上一个单元的录影。在看到书的标志 ▶️ 时，就停下录影带，打开你的练习手册。依次完成所有练习，直到你看见录影的标志 🔲 时为止。这时候你可继续观看录影直到你又看到书的标志 ▶️ 为止。每一单元，在看听说部分后有练习，在跟着念部分后也有练习，然后在真实人生、真实语言部分以后又有练习。请记住：只要你看到书的标志 ▶️ ，就打开练习手册作练习；每当你在练习手册中看到录影的标志 🔲 时，就回头再看录影带。

在作完练习手册中的所有练习以后，你应该重看一遍该单元的录影。比较一下，看你现在比你第一次看这一单元时是否懂得更多了--参照你当时写下的小结，就可知道你当时看懂了多少。随着课程的进展，你会发现你写的小结也越来越准确。

三．听说

在看完录影带，作完练习以后，你就可以使用配套的录音带进行实际的演练。随时有空，只要把录音带放进你的随身听或音响设备就可反复练习--如在上班的路上，作家务的时候，只要有十分钟的空闲就足够了。

把注意力集中在发音上。如果你的发音不是十全十美也没什么关系。只要经常练习，你就会有所提高。不少美国人都带有一定的口音，但大家还是能够交流。在观看录影带的时候，你也会注意到乔治、爱莉拉、敏和沙夏都带有外国口音，但他们都能沟通，这也就达到了目的。

课程资料

• 一盘六十分钟录影带

在 "新移民英语" 系列的录影带中，你将结识赛门和瑞其尔，他们是一对伴侣，在国际中心作义工，协助和指导象你这样的新移民，帮助他们适应在美国的生活。你还会结识从墨西哥来的乔治和爱莉拉夫妇，俄国来的油漆工沙夏以及从香港来的女侍敏，敏梦想有一天会自己开餐馆。欢迎你加入他们的行列，赛门和瑞其尔即是他们的指导，也可作你的指导。

录影由七个单元组成，每个单元针对一个实际的情景。每一单元包括三个部分：

Hear it, See it, Say it (看听说)
在这一部分，你将学习与本单元主题有关的主要词汇。你会听到词汇的发音，理解它的意思，看到它的英文拼写并跟着重复生词。

Watch and Listen (跟着念)
这一部分是每一单元的核心。你将看到和听到与本单元有关的语句。在这一部分结束时，你会听到重要短语的简要复习。

Real People...Real Language (真实人生...真实语言)
这一部分是真人真事的采访，被采访的人将告诉你他们在美国的生活情况。这样你有机会听到和练习真实的语言。每单元的各部分都在前一部分的基础上延伸，语言难度也逐渐加深，这样每一单元你都会有所进步！而且，你听到的英语都是真实生活中使用的语言，使你能够明白区域或外国口音，从而在日常生活中进行应用。

• 一百四十四页的练习手册

练习手册中的练习将帮助你扩大词汇，学习基本英文规则及应用。手册还有主要概念的简短说明。要求你作的练习大致包括以下内容：

☞ 说出你在录影中看到的人和物

☞ 填写动词时态

☞ 用"是"或"不是"回答问题

☞ 多种选择题

☞ 完成句子或回答问题

☞ 填空

每个练习的头一题或头两题是示范题，教你作题的方法。所有练习答案都可在书后答案一节内找到。

练习手册中的每个单元之后，都附有完整的录影原稿。此外，书末还附有课程中使用的所有单词表。

• 录音带

看完录影和作完练习手册中的所有练习以后，你就可以利用录音带来复习和演练你刚学过的课程。先听母语为英文的人复习你在录影和练习手册中见过单词和短语，然后跟着他们重复。你同时还要演练问答，用词造句替换单词。他们每次都会先给你示范，教你演练的方法，然后才让你来作答。稍候片刻，你就会听到正确的答案。录音带也是一个练习发音的特好办法。

• 录音原稿

可随身携带的录音原稿包括你在录音带上听到的所有内容。你可以从原稿中查找你不明白的词汇或短语的写法。

让我们现在就开始吧。

서론

Living Language® 에서는 외국어 공부를 위한 연재 기획물의 일환으로 *English for New Americans* 을 제작하였습니다. *English for New Americans* 은 "살아있는" 영어를 이해하고 회화를 하는 능력을 항상 시켜 줄 것입니다. 완성코스는 이 학습서와 60분 짜리 비디오카세트, 60분 짜리 오디오 카세트와 오디오 교재로 구성되어 있습니다.

English for New Americans 프로그램은 집중 훈련 식이므로, 일상생활에 도입하여 처음부터 영어를 구사할 수 있게 해 드립니다. 이 프로그램은, 필요한 단어, 숙어, 기초 문법과 같은 도구를 제공하여 미국에서의 전형적인 상황에서 대화할 수 있게 도와줍니다.

프로그램 사용 방법

English for New Americans 의 1-2-3 방법은 사용하기 쉽게 되어 있습니다.

I. 비디오를 잘 보십시오.
비디오 테이프를 VCR에 넣고 편안하게 앉아서 각 편을 처음부터 끝까지 보십시오. 처음 볼 때 모든 말을 이해하지 못하여도 걱정하지 마십시오. 다음 번에 또 볼 기회가 있습니다. 바디 랭귀지나 얼굴 표정 그리고 주변환경에 주의를 기울이십시오. 그러면 이미 얼마나 이해를 할 수 있는지 놀라실 것입니다. 처음 본 후 "보고 듣기" 편에서 무슨 일이 일어났다고 생각하는지를 간략하게 적어 두셔도 됩니다. 비디오 한 편을 완전히 보신 후, 비디오를 그 편의 처음으로 다시 감으십시오.

2. 다시 보십시오. 학습서를 읽고 쓰십시오.
같은 편을 다시 보십시오. 스크린에서 ▶▉표를 보면, 테이프를 중단하고 학습서를 펴십시오. ▣▣ 표가 나올 때까지 순서대로 연습문제를 끝내십시오. 그런 후 다음 ▶▉ 표가 나올 때까지 비디오를 다시 보십시오. 매 편마다, "보고 듣고 말하기", "보고 듣기" 그리고 "실제 인물, 현지 언어" 순서대로 연습문제를 끝내도록 해야 합니다. ▶▉ 표를 보면 언제나 학습서로 가고, 학습서에서 ▣▣ 표를 보면 비디오로 돌아가는 것을 잊지 마십시오.

학습서에 있는 연습 문제를 모두 끝낸 후, 비디오를 한 번 더 보십시오. 이번에는 처음보다 얼마나 더 이해할 수 있었는지를 비교하십시오. 적어 둔 요약을 보십시오. 처음엔 얼마나 이해했습니까? 프로그램이 진행됨에 실제 얼마나 진보하고 있는지 알게 될 것입니다.

3. 듣고 말하기

비디오를 공부하기와 학습서의 연습문제를 끝낸 후, 배운 것을 오디오 카세트로
연습할 수 있습니다. 카세트를 녹음기에 넣고, 집에서나, 출근할 때나,
집안 일을 할 때 등, 어디서나 10분 정도의 시간이 있는 편한 시간에,
듣고 따라 하십시오.

말소리에 귀를 기울이십시오. 액센트가 완벽하게 되지 않아도 걱정하지
마십시오. 연습을 많이 할수록 향상 될 것입니다. 그리고 미국에서는 사람들이
여러 종류의 액센트로 얘기하고 있지만, 모두들 의사 전달을 할 수 있습니다.
비디오에서 보시겠지만, Jorge, Elena, Ming 그리고 Sasha 는 모두 외국 액센트가
있지만 의사 소통을 할 수 있습니다. 바로 그것에 뜻이 있는 것입니다!

재료
• 60 분 짜리 비디오카세트
English for New Americans 비디오 시리즈에서는, Simon 과 Raquel 이라는
남녀가 인터네쇼날 센터에 자원하여 새로운 이민자들이 미국생활에 적응할 수
있도록 조언을 해 줍니다. 또한, 멕시코에서 온 부부인 Jorge 와 Elena, 쏘련
칠장이인 Sasha, 자신의 레스트랑을 차리고 싶다는 꿈을 가지고 홍콩에서 온
웨이트레스 Ming 등이 비디오에 등장합니다. 그들과 함께 하시지 않겠습니까?
Simon 과 Raquel이 여러분의 가이드가 되어 드릴 것입니다.

이 비디오는 7 편이며 매 편이 일상생활로 구성되어 있습니다. 매편은 세가지
항목으로 되어 있습니다.

Hear It, See It, Say It (듣고, 보고, 말하기)
이 편에서는 주어진 토픽에 관련된 중요 단어가 소개됩니다. 단어를 어떻게
발음하며, 뜻이 무엇이며, 영어로 어떻게 스펠링을 쓰는지 듣게 됩니다. 새로운
단어마다 따라 하십시오.

Watch and Listen (보고 듣기)
이 편은 각 항목의 심장부입니다. 매 편의 토픽에 관련된 말을 보고, 들을
것입니다.

Real People...Real Language (실제 인물-- 현지 언어)
이 편은 실제 인물들이 미국에서의 생활을 얘기하는 인터뷰로 구성되어
있습니다. 이것은 실지 언어를 듣고 연습할 기회를 줍니다. 매 편의 각 항목은
전 편에 연결되어, 언어가 더욱 흥미 있어지며, 매 편마다 발전하는 것을 느낄 수
있을 것입니다. 그보다도, 실제로 말하는대로의 영어를 들을 수 있어서,
지방 액센트나 외국 액센트를 알아듣고 일상생활에 사용할 수 있게 됩니다.

• 144 페이지의 학습서

학습서에는, 중요 문법개념의 설명과 단어 실력 향상, 영어의 기본 법칙과
적용방법에 대한 것을 배우실 것입니다. 이 학습서에서 중요개념의 간략한
설명을 볼 수 있을 것입니다. 여기서는 아래와 같은 문제에 대답해야 합니다:

☞ 비디오에서 본 사물과 사람의 이름

☞ 정확한 동사 변형 넣기

☞ "yes" 와 "no"로 질문에 대답하기

☞ 정답 취사 선택하기

☞ 문장의 첫 부분과 끝 부분 맞추기와, 질문을 대답으로 끝내기

☞ 공백난에 정답 넣기

처음 한 두 문제는 대답을 대신 해 보일 것입니다. 책 뒤의 Answer Key 에
답안이 모두 있습니다.

비디오에서 보고 들은 문장의 완전한 교재가 학습서 각 편 끝에 수록되어 있습니다.
그리고, 책 뒷면에서는 프로그램에 사용된 모든 단어를 찾을 수 있습니다.

• 오디오 카세트

일단 비디오의 한 편을 보고 학습서에 있는 연습문제를 끝내면,
오디오 카세트를 사용하여 배운 것을 복습하고 연습할 수 있습니다.
비디오에서 들은 것과 학습서에서 본 단어와 문장을 현지 미국인이
복습하는 것을 듣고 따라하십시오. 스스로 문장을 만들고, 단어를 변경하고,
문장을 바꾸어서 질문하고 대답하는 연습을 할 것입니다. 언제나
어떻게 해야하는지 샘플을 먼저 들은 다음 대답하십시오. 그리고 잠시 후
정답을 들을 것입니다. 이 오디오 카세트는 발음 연습하기에도 아주 좋은
방법입니다.

• 오디오 대본

포켓 사이즈의 오디오 대본에는 오디오 카세트에서 들은 모든 문장 교재가 포함
되어 있습니다. 이해하지 못했던 단어를 찾을 수 있고, 문장이 어떻게
쓰여졌는지 찾아 볼 수 있습니다.

자, 그럼 시작합시다.

ВВЕДЕНИЕ

Разрешите познакомить вас с серией языковых учебных программ *English for New Americans*, подготовленных фирмой Living Language®. *English for New Americans*: Everyday Life позволит вам заметно улучшить свои способности говорить и понимать на «реальном» американском английском языке. Полный курс состоит из этого пособия, одной 60-минутной видеокассеты, одной 60-минутной аудиокассеты и аудиосценария.

В основу программы *English for New Americans* положен подход погружения, поэтому вы с самого начала будете пользоваться английским языком, как бы вы делали это в реальной жизни. Программа предоставляет вам все необходимые инструменты – словарь, фразы, а также основы грамматики, - с тем чтобы помочь вам в общении в рамках типичных ситуаций, которые могут возникнуть в вашей повседневной жизни в Соединенных Штатах. Мы рекомендовали бы вам также приобрести для работы хороший словарь.

КАК ПОЛЬЗОВАТЬСЯ ЭТОЙ ПРОГРАММОЙ

Используемый в программе *English for New Americans* метод 1-2-3 существенно облегчает ее применение.

1. ПРОСМОТРИТЕ ВИДЕОПРОГРАММУ

Возьмите видеокассету, включите видеопроигрыватель, удобно сядьте и просмотрите всю программу полностью. Не волнуйтесь, если вы с первого раза всего не поймете. У вас есть возможность просмотреть программу снова. В ходе просмотра обращайте внимание на выражение лиц, телодвижения и окружающую обстановку. Вы будете просто поражены тем, как много вы уже понимаете! После первого сеанса просмотра попробуйте написать краткое резюме того, что, как вы считаете, происходило в разделе Watch and Listen. После чего перемотайте пленку.

2. ПРОСМОТРИТЕ СНОВА, СДЕЛАЙТЕ УПРАЖНЕНИЯ ПО ЧТЕНИЮ И ПИСЬМУ, КОТОРЫЕ ПРИВЕДЕНЫ В ПОСОБИИ

Вновь просмотрите эту же часть. Когда вы видите появляющийся на экране значок ▶▮ , останавливайте просмотр и обращайтесь к пособию. Продолжайте выполнять упражнения, следуя указаниям, до того момента, пока вы не увидите значок ▬▬ . Затем вновь приступайте к просмотру видеоматериала, пока не увидите на экране очередной значок ▶▮ . В каждой части вам будет предлагаться сделать ряд упражнений после раздела See it, Hear it, Say it, идущего после раздела Watch and Listen, который в свою очередь следует за разделом Real People, Real Language. Запомните: как только вы видите значок ▶▮ , переходите к пособию; как только в пособии вы видите значок ▬▬ , возвращайтесь к просмотру видеоматериала.

После того, как вы закончите выполнение всех упражнений из пособия, просмотрите видеоматериал еще раз. Попробуйте сравнить насколько лучше вы понимаете материал в этот раз, по сравнению с первым разом! Посмотрите написанное вами резюме – сколько вам удалось понять? По мере дальнейшего просмотра программы вы будете все реальнее ощущать тот прогресс, которого вам удалось добиться.

3. СЛУШАЙТЕ И ПОВТОРЯЙТЕ

После того, как вы закончили просмотр видео и сделали все упражнения из пособия, вы можете попробовать использовать на практике то, что вы уже выучили с помощью аудиокассеты. Вставьте кассету в магнитофон и слушайте и повторяйте услышанное везде, где это удобно – дома, по пути на работу, во время выполнения обязанностей по хозяйству или в любое другое время, когда у вас появилось 10 свободных минут.

Особое внимание уделяйте звуковому оформлению языковых ситуаций. Пусть вас не волнует, если у вас не совсем идеальное произношение. Чем больше вы будете практиковаться, тем заметнее будут ваши результаты. Кроме того, в Соединенных Штатах люди говорят с самыми разнообразными акцентами, однако всем удается общаться. Вы увидите в ходе просмотра видео, что Джордж, Елена, Минг и Саша говорят с иностранным акцентом, но они в состоянии объясниться, а именно это самое главное!

МАТЕРИАЛЫ
• ОДНА 60-МИНУТНАЯ ВИДЕОКАССЕТА

В ходе просмотра видеоматериалов серий English for New Americans вы повстречаетесь с парой - Саймон и Рэкел, которые на добровольных началах работают в международном центре, помогая таким как вы новым иммигрантам и консультируя их по мере того, как они вливаются в повседневную жизнь в Соединенных Штатах. Вы также познакомитесь с Джорджем и Еленой, супружеской парой из Мексики, Сашей, маляром их России, и Минг, официанткой из Гонконга с амбициозными планами открыть свой собственный ресторан. Присоединяйтесь к ним! А Саймон и Рэкел станут как их, так и вашими гидами.

Этот видеоматериал состоит из семи частей, в каждой из которых дается описание какой-либо конкретной ситуации. Каждая часть состоит из трех разделов:

Hear it, See it, Say it (Посмотри это, послушай это, скажи это)
В этом разделе вы познакомитесь с ключевыми словами по теме данной части. Вы услышите произношение слова, увидите, что оно обозначает, а также увидите, как оно пишется по-английски. Повторяйте каждое выученное вами новое слово.

Watch and Listen (Смотри и слушай)
Этот раздел является как бы сердцевиной каждой части. Вы сможете увидеть и

услышать языковые материалы, касающиеся тематики данной части. В конце раздела вы услышите краткий обзор нескольких важных фраз.

Real People...Real Language (Настоящие люди ... настоящий язык)
В этом разделе содержатся интервью с реальными людьми, которые расскажут вам о своей жизни в Соединенных Штатах. Это дает вам возможность слушать и употреблять на практике реальный язык. Каждый раздел части построен с учетом предыдущего материала, язык становится более сложным, поэтому вы увидите, как вы прогрессируете с каждой новой частью! Кроме того, вы услышите английский язык в его реальном произношении, что позволит вам понимать региональные говоры и иностранные акценты, а также использовать то, что вы выучили в повседневной жизни.

• ПОСОБИЕ НА 144 СТРАНИЦАХ

В этом пособии вы сможете найти упражнения, которые помогут вам создать собственный словарный запас, выучить основные правила английского языка и научиться ими пользоваться. Также вы найдете краткие толкования ключевых концепций. Возможно, вам будет предложено сделать следующее:

- назвать объект или лицо, увиденные вами при просмотре видеоматериалов
- поставить глагол в правильную форму
- ответить «да» или «нет» на поставленные вопросы
- выбрать из нескольких предложенных правильный вариант ответа
- подобрать к началу предложения соответствующее окончание или к вопросу - ответ
- вставить пропущенную информацию.

На один- два первых вопроса в каждом из упражнений будут даны ответы с тем, чтобы показать вам, что нужно делать. Все ответы вы сможете найти в конце книги в Указателе ответов.

В конце каждой части пособия вы найдете полный сценарий того, что вы видели и слышали на видео. Кроме того, в конце книги дается список слов, где вы можете найти все слова, которые употреблялись в этой программе.

• ОДНА 60-МИНУТНАЯ АУДИО КАССЕТА

После того, как вы просмотрите видеоматериал и сделаете упражнения из пособия, вы можете прослушать аудиокассету, чтобы проверить, что вы уже выучили и поупражняться с выученным материалом. Просто слушайте и повторяйте за говорящими на родном языке те слова и фразы, которые вы услышали в видеоматериале и встретили в пособии. Кроме того, ваша практика предполагает, что вы будете задавать вопросы и отвечать на них, составлять собственные предложения, а также изменять структуру предложений, заменяя одно слово другим. Постоянно звучат примеры, которые говорят вам, что нужно делать, после чего наступает ваша очередь отвечать. А затем, после краткой паузы, вы слышите правильный вариант ответа. Более того, аудиокассета станет для вас серьезным подспорьем в практике произношения!

• АУДИО СЦЕНАРИЙ

Аудио сценарий карманного размера содержит полный текст услышанного вами материала аудиокассеты. В нем вы можете найти значения слов, которых вы не понимаете, или посмотреть написание отдельных фраз.

Итак, давайте начнем...

Unit 1
At the International Center: Introductions

A. Introductions

Write the word.

1. Hello.

2. How ____are____ you?

3. _____ , thanks.

4. And _____ ?

5. _____ is Ming.

6. Nice to _____ you.

7. This _____ Jorge.

8. _____ pleasure.

B. Countries

Write the country.

1. Hong Kong, ____China____

2. Moscow, _____

3. New York, _____

4. Mexico City, _____

C. Professions

Where do they work?

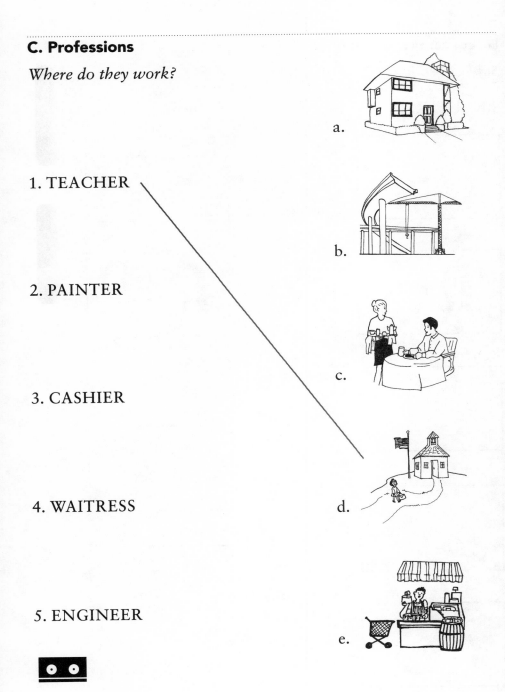

1. TEACHER

2. PAINTER

3. CASHIER

4. WAITRESS

5. ENGINEER

D. Verbs: Present Tense—*To Be*

Subject Pronouns

SINGULAR   PLURAL

 I   we

 you   you

 he

 she   they

 it

SINGULAR		PLURAL	
I	am	we	are
you	are	you	are
he	is	they	are
she	is	they	are
it	is	they	are

yesterday	today	tomorrow

PRESENT

Write the verbs in the sentences.

1. Simon _____ **is** _____ at the International Center.

2. Jorge and Elena _____ from Mexico.

3. Raquel _____ Simon's wife.

4. Jorge _____ Elena's husband.

5. Ming _____ a waitress.

6. Sasha _____ from Russia.

7. Raquel and Jorge _____ hungry.

8. I _____ hungry, too.

9. We _____ at home.

10. You _____ a teacher.

E. Contractions

I am = I'm
you are = you're
he is = he's
she is = she's
it is = it's

we are = we're
you are = you're
they are = they're

21

Write the contractions.

1. you are = __you're__

2. they are = _____

3. it is = _____

4. I am = _____

5. we are = _____

6. he is = _____

F. Negatives

Simon is a teacher. He **is not** a painter.

Raquel is a social worker. She **is not** an engineer.

I am not		**we are not**	
you are not		**you are not**	
he is not			
she is not		**they are not**	
it is not			

Write the negative form of the verb.

1. I __am not__ at the International Center.

2. Simon and Raquel __are not__ at home.

3. Ming _____ an engineer.

4. Elena _____ hungry.

5. Sasha _____ from Mexico.

6. Jorge _____ a teacher.

7. You _____ a social worker.

8. Elena and Jorge _____ from Russia.

9. We _____ on vacation.

10. The food _____ on the table.

G. Negative Contractions

I'm not	we're not / we aren't
you're not / you aren't	you're not / you aren't
he's not / he isn't	
she's not / she isn't	they're not / they aren't
it's not / it isn't	

Write the contractions.

1. he is not = **he's not/he isn't**

2. they are not = _____

3. we are not = _____

4. I am not = _____

5. you are not = _____

6. she is not = _____

H. Questions and Yes/No Answers

Jorge is an engineer. Is Jorge an engineer? **Yes, he is.**

Elena is a cashier. Is Elena a waitress? **No, she is not.**

Write a "yes" or "no" short answer after the question.

1. Is Sasha from the Dominican Republic? **No, he is not.**

2. Is he from Russia? **Yes, he is.**

3. Is Raquel from the Dominican Republic? **Yes,** _____

4. Are you from the United States? **No,** _____

5. Are Jorge and Elena from the United States? **No,** _____

Change the sentence to a question.

6. Simon is from the United States.

_____ **Is Simon from the United States?** _____

7. You are from Hong Kong.

_____

8. Sasha and Ming are at the International Center.

_____

9. Elena and Jorge are hungry.

_____

10. The food is on the table.

_____

I. Question Words

Who?   What?   Where?

*Write **Who, What,** or **Where** in the question.*

1. _____ **Who** _____ is at the International Center? —Simon and Raquel are.

2. _____ is with Simon and Raquel? —Jorge, Elena, Sasha, and Ming are.

3. _____ is on the table? —The food is.

4. _____ is with you? —My friends are.

5. _____ are the children? —In school.

6. _____ is Sasha? —A painter.

7. _____ are you? —At home.

8. _____ are you? —A student.

J. Short Answers

Circle the correct short answer to the question.

1. **Who** is from China?   (Ming is.)   Elena is.

2. **Where** are Jorge and Elena from? From Colombia. From Mexico.

3. **Who** is from Russia?   Raquel is.   Sasha is.

4. **Where** is Raquel from?   From the U.S.   From the D.R.

5. **Who** is from the United States? Sasha is.   Simon is.

K. Country/Nationality/Language

I am from <u>Brazil</u>.   I am <u>Brazilian</u>.   I speak <u>Portuguese</u>.
   (country)   (nationality)   (language)

Fill in the chart with a country, nationality, or language.

	Country	Nationality	Language
1.	Brazil	Brazilian	**Portuguese**
2.	Dominican Republic		Spanish
3.		Chinese	Chinese
4.	Haiti	Haitian	French
5.	Japan	Japanese	Japanese

6.	Korea	Korean	Korean
7.	Mexico		Spanish
8.	Russia		Russian
9.	United States		English
10.	Vietnam	Vietnamese	Vietnamese

L. People/Countries

Write a country, nationality, or language in the sentence.

1. Raquel is from the **Dominican Republic**. She's Dominican.

2. Ming is from China. She's _____.

3. Elena and Jorge are from _____. They're Mexican.

4. Sasha is from Russia. He's _____.

5. Simon is from the _____. He's American.

6. Raquel, Jorge, and Elena speak English and _____.

7. Sasha speaks English and _____.

8. Ming speaks English and _____.

9. Simon speaks only _____!

M. Dialogue

Read the dialogue and fill in the missing words.

1. SIMON: Hi! My name is **Simon**.

2. JORGE: Nice to meet _____.

   This _____ Elena.

3. ELENA: Pleased to _____ you.

4. SIMON: _____ pleasure.

5. RAQUEL: I'd like to introduce _____ to Ming.

6. MING: _____ to meet you.

7. SIMON: How are _____?

8. RAQUEL: And _____ is Sasha.

9. JORGE: Nice to _____ you.

10. SASHA: My _____.

11. JORGE: _____ you hungry?

_____ am. Let's eat!

N. Professions and Workplaces

Make a word from the letters for a person who works in this place.

1. (CREETAH)

A **teacher** works in a school.

3. (SATISREW)

A _____ works in a restaurant.

2. (RESHICA)

A _____ works in a store.

4. (GERNINEE)

An _____ works for a company.

O. Real People...Real Language

Circle the word you hear.

1. Paul   (computer)   collector
2. Jen   student   secretary
3. Shin   Thailand   Taiwan
4. Eleonor   consultant   college
5. Consuelo   American   Mexican
6. Anna   Ukraine   Uruguay
7. Yao Li   Tai Chi   Taipei
8. Manuel   Colorado   Colombia
9. Liz   mother   math teacher
10. Sandra   Port au Prince   Puerto Rico
11. Susan   Jamaica   Georgia
12. Ken   technology   telephone

VIDEO TRANSCRIPT

Watch and Listen

Simon: Today we're having a party at the International Center. We're going to meet some people and introduce ourselves. Come and join us!... Jorge! Hello, how are you?

Jorge: Fine, thank you. And you?

Simon: Very well, thank you.

Jorge: I'd like to introduce my wife, Elena.

Simon: Pleased to meet you.

Elena: My pleasure.

Simon: And this is my lovely wife, Raquel.

Jorge: Nice to meet you.

Elena: Nice to meet you.

Raquel: I'd like you to meet Ming.

Simon: Pleased to meet you, Ming.

Ming: How do you do?

Raquel: Ming is from Hong Kong. She's a waitress.

Simon: Oh, really? Where?

Ming: In the Golden Garden Restaurant.

Simon: We'll have to go there for dinner sometime.

Raquel: That's a good idea. And this is Sasha.

Simon: How are you?

Sasha: Nice to meet you.

Simon: Where are you from, Sasha?

Sasha: I'm from Russia.

Simon: And what do you do?

Sasha: I'm a painter—I paint houses.

Simon: That's a very useful profession!

Sasha: And what do you do?

Raquel: Well, I'm a social worker and Simon's an English teacher.

Simon: And, Jorge, what about you?

Jorge: I'm an engineer.

Raquel: And where are you from?

Elena: We're from Mexico.

Simon: Chinese, Russian, Mexican. This truly is the International Center.

Elena: And what about you?

Raquel: Simon is American, and I'm Dominican. We met on vacation.

Ming: Oh, that sounds romantic!

Simon: It was. So, is anybody hungry?

Raquel: Yes—let's eat!

Jorge: Yes, let's eat!

Simon: While they're eating, let's review some useful phrases you've just heard.

To introduce yourself, say:

> **Hi, I'm...**   or
>
> **My name is...**

To introduce someone else, say:

> **I'd like you to meet...**   or
>
> **This is...**

To answer, you can say,

> **Nice to meet you.**   or
>
> **My pleasure.**

Now let's meet some more people.

Unit 2
A City Tour:
The Time and Date

A. Days, Months, and Seasons

Write the days on the calendar.

1.

JANUARY						
Sunday						
1	2	3	4	5	6	7
8	8	10	11	12	13	14
15	16	17	18	19	20	21
22	23	24	25	26	27	28
29	30	31				

Write the months of the year after the seasons.

2. SPRING M **March**
S A APRIL
M MAY

4. FALL S **September**
O OCTOBER
N November

3. SUMMER J **June**
S J July
A August

5. WINTER **December**
D JANUARY
D I
F FEBRUARY

32

B. Verbs: Present Continuous—*To Be* + ___*ing*

work + ing = working   come + ing = coming

go + ing = going   write + ing = writing

I	am ___ing	we	are ___ing
you	are ___ing	you	are ___ing
he	is ___ing		
she	is ___ing	they	are ___ing
it	is ___ing		

Contractions: I am = I'm; you are = you're; etc.

yesterday   today   tomorrow

present continuous:
now
at the moment

Write the verbs in the sentences.

1. Raquel _____**is waiting**_____ at the International Center. (wait)

2. Ming _____**is coming**_____ on the tour. (come)

3. They _____ about the weekend. (talk)

4. Raquel _____ Ming the time. (ask)

5. Ming _____ at her watch. (look)

6. Ming _____ Raquel the time. (tell)

7. Sasha _____ to the center. (walk)

8. They _____ to the library. (go)

9. We _____ the verbs. (write)

10. I _____ this exercise. (finish)

C. Negative

I	am not ___ ing		
you	are not ___ ing	we	are not ___ ing
he	is not ___ ing	you	are not ___ ing
she	is not ___ ing	they	are not ___ ing
it	is not ___ ing		

Write the negative form of the verb.

1. Simon _____**is not going**_____ on the tour. (go)

2. Sasha _____ at the International Center. (wait)

3. Ming and Raquel _____. (shop*)

4. Jorge _____ a birthday party. (have)

5. Elena _____ to Raquel. (talk)

6. My friends _____ on the bus. (sit*)

7. I _____ now. (get* up)

8. You _____ dinner now. (eat)

9. We _____ TV. (watch)

10. The cat _____ on the bed. (sleep)

* Notice: shop + ing = sho<u>pp</u>ing; sit + ing = si<u>tt</u>ing; get + ing = ge<u>tt</u>ing

D. Yes/No Answers

Write a "yes" or "no" short answer after the question.

1. Is Raquel waiting for some people? __**Yes, she is.**__

2. Is Jorge getting up? __**No, he isn't.**__

3. Is Ming's birthday this week? __**Yes,**_____

4. Are Sasha and Ming going on the tour? **Yes,** _____

5. Is it a beautiful day? **Yes,** _____

6. Are Jorge and Elena at the center? **No,** _____

7. Is it almost ten o'clock? **Yes,** _____

8. Are Ming's weekends fun? **Yes,** _____

9. Is Sasha late? **No,** _____

10. Is the library open? **Yes,** _____

E. Question Words

When?

Which?

*Write **When** or **Which** in the questions.*

1. ____**When**____ is your birthday? —In June.

2. _____ season is your favorite? —Fall is.

3. _____ are you going to bed? —At 11:00.

4. _____ day is today? —It's Saturday.

5. _____ is the baseball game? —At 7:00.

6. _____ is your summer vacation? —In August.

7. _____ are they going on the tour? —At 10:00.

8. _____ days are you working? —On Monday and Friday.

9. _____ is the movie showing? —This weekend.

F. Prepositions of Time

in	January the summer the morning / the afternoon / the evening
on	Monday / Tuesday afternoon June second
at	9:00 / noon night

Write in, on, or at in the sentences.

1. Sasha is going to a movie ___at___ 3:30 ___in___ the afternoon.

2. I'm visiting my family _____ December.

3. Raquel is working at the center _____ Tuesday and Thursday.

4. We are in the cafeteria _____ noon.

5. They are getting married _____ July 6th (sixth).

6. Ming is finishing work _____ 10:30 _____ night.

7. You are going on vacation _____ July.

8. Jorge and Elena are going to a restaurant _____ Friday.

9. The weather is beautiful in this part of the country _____ the fall.

10. Simon's birthday is _____ October 17th (seventeenth).

G. Dialogue

Choose the missing words.

SIMON: Hi! I'm ___sorry___ I'm late.
1. (sorry/happy)

RAQUEL: That's all _____. Jorge and Elena are
                          2. (right/wrong)

            meeting us at the movie theater _____ 7:00.
                                                 3. (in/at)

            We have half an hour.

SIMON: Oh good. _____ a nice dress!
                        4. (Who/What)

RAQUEL: Thank _____. I went shopping today.
                     5. (me/you)

SIMON: What _____ we doing this weekend?
                      6. (are/is)

RAQUEL: I don't know.

SIMON: _____ go for a drive in the country
              7. (Let's/What's)

            _____ Sunday afternoon.
                8. (at/on)

RAQUEL: That's a great idea! The trees are beautiful in the

            _____ .
                9. (winter/fall)

H. Number Practice

Practice saying these numbers.

1 one	11 eleven	21 twenty-one	40 forty
2 two	12 twelve	22 twenty-two	50 fifty
3 three	13 thirteen	23 twenty-three	60 sixty
4 four	14 fourteen	24 twenty-four	70 seventy
5 five	15 fifteen	25 twenty-five	80 eighty
6 six	16 sixteen	26 twenty-six	90 ninety
7 seven	17 seventeen	27 twenty-seven	100 one hundred
8 eight	18 eighteen	28 twenty-eight	101 one hundred and one
9 nine	19 nineteen	29 twenty-nine	200 two hundred
10 ten	20 twenty	30 thirty	1000 one thousand

Note: A.M. = 12:00 midnight – 12:00 noon = 00:00 – 11:59
P.M. = 12:00 noon – 12:00 midnight = 12:00 – 23:59

I. Telling Time

Write the time in numbers.

What time is it?

1. **1:10**   2. _____   3. _____   4. _____

What's the time?

5. _____   6. _____   7. _____   8. _____

Do you have the time?

9. _____   10. _____   11. _____   12. _____

Write the time in letters.

1. **It's one-ten.**   7. _____

2. **It's two-twenty-five.**   8. _____

3. _____   9. _____

4. _____   10. _____

5. _____   11. _____

6. _____   12. _____

J. What's the Date?

JANUARY						
SUNDAY	MONDAY	TUESDAY	WEDNESDAY	THURSDAY	FRIDAY	SATURDAY
1	2	3	4	5	6	7
8	8	10	11	12	13	14
15	16	17	18	19	20	21
22	23	24	25	26	27	28
29	30	31				

Write the day in the sentences.

1. January **fifth** is a ___Thursday___.

2. January **tenth** is a _____.

3. January **eighteenth** is a _____.

4. January **twenty-seventh** is a _____.

5. January **thirtieth** is a _____.

K. Real People...Real Language

1. What time do you go to work?

Check the time you hear.

a. 8:00 _____   8:30 _____✔_____

b. 7:00 _____   7:30 _____

c. 8:00 _____   8:15 _____

d. 7:00 _____   11:00 _____

e. 7:00 _____   11:00 _____

f. 6:00 _____   8:00 _____

g. 5:00 _____   9:00 _____

2. When is your birthday? Do you have a party?

Draw a line from the date to the party.

a. October 7th   no party

b. July 3rd   dinner in a restaurant

c. June   stopped having parties

d. October 24th   dinner and phone calls

e. November 9th   party with family and friends

3. What's your favorite season?

Write the season.

a. _____**summer**_____ baseball

b. _____ snowboarding

c. _____ love the heat and swimming

d. _____ change of colors and riding

e. _____ not too hot, not too cold

f. _____ enjoy being outside

g. _____ sailing and golf

VIDEO TRANSCIPT

Watch and Listen

Raquel: Okay, as soon as everyone gets here, we'll get started.

Ming: Hi, Raquel! Am I the first one here?

Raquel: Yes, you are. How was your weekend?

Ming: It was nice. On Saturday I went shopping, and on Sunday I went to a movie.

Raquel: Sounds like a fun weekend!

Ming: How about you?

Raquel: Saturday we went to a baseball game, and Sunday was Simon's birthday.

Ming: Really? My birthday is October 20th.

Raquel: That's Wednesday. Happy birthday!

Ming: Thank you.

Raquel: What time is it?

Ming: It's 9:45.

Raquel: It's still early.

Ming: Who else is coming?

Raquel: Sasha and maybe some others.

Ming: What a beautiful day for a tour!

Raquel: Yeah, fall is beautiful in this part of the country…Where is everyone?

Sasha: What time is it? Am I late?

Raquel: No, it's almost ten o'clock. You're just in time.

Sasha: Good. I got up late this morning.

Raquel: Sasha, you remember Ming.

Sasha: Yes, we met last week.

Ming: We met at the party here.

Raquel: That's right. Well, let's get started. We'll start with the city library. They open at ten o'clock...But before we go, here are some phrases to remember from this lesson.

If you are sorry about something, you can say:

       I'm sorry I'm late.   or

       I didn't mean to miss your party.

People might reply:

       That's all right.   or

       Don't worry about it.

If you are surprised or pleased about something, you can say:

       What a nice car!   or

       What cute kids!

Now, let's listen to some people talk about their schedules: at what time they do things, on which days, and during which months.

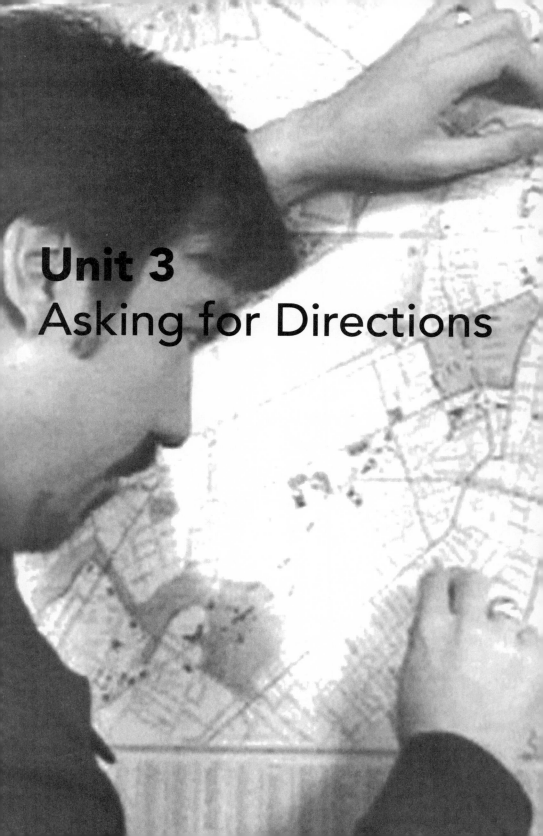

Unit 3
Asking for Directions

A. What is it?

Write the missing word on the line.

1. BUS __STOP__   2. MAIL _____

3. _____ OFFICE   4. _____ THEATER

B. Odd One Out

Cross out the word that does not belong.

1.	get on	bus	get off	bus stop	~~letter~~
2.	subway	stamp	machine	token	train
3.	movie	turn left	go straight	turn right	cross the street
4.	letter	stamp	theater	mailbox	post office

C. Opposites

Write the opposite word on the line.

1. Turn left.   ≠   Turn __right__.

2. Get on.   ≠   Get _____.

3. It s near.   ≠   It's _____.

4. It s here.   ≠   It's _____.

44

D. Verbs: Simple Present

SINGULAR		PLURAL	
I	sit	we	sit
you	sit	you	sit
he/she/it	sits	they	sit

yesterday   today   tomorrow

PRESENT

always
usually
sometimes
never

Also use the simple present tense with these words:

	day		Mondays		March
every	week	**on**	weekends	**in**	winter
	year		my birthday		the morning

Write the verbs in the sentences.

1. Simon ____**sits**____ at the information desk every week. (sit)

2. He _____ questions. (answer)

3. Elena _____ Simon for directions. (ask)

4. She _____ to go to the supermarket. (want)

5. Jorge _____ some stamps. (need)

6. He _____ the bus to the post office. (take)

7. Elena and Jorge _____ near the International Center. (live)

8. We _____ in a restaurant once a week. (eat)

9. You _____ English well. (speak)

10. I _____ every day. (study)

E. Negatives

I	do not speak	we	do not speak
you	do not speak	you	do not speak
he / she / it	does not speak	they	do not speak

Contractions: I do not = I don't; he does not = he doesn't; etc.

Write the negative form of the verb.

1. Jorge ___**doesn't speak**___ Russian. (speak)

2. Elena _____ a car. (drive)

3. Ming _____ in a bank. (work)

4. Simon and Raquel _____ to work
   by train. (go)

5. Sasha _____ pictures. (paint)

6. I _____ your friends. (know)

7. You _____ tea for breakfast. (drink)

8. We _____ medicine at that pharmacy.
   (buy)

9. They _____ movies during
   the week. (watch)

10. The cat _____ meat, only fish. (eat)

F. Yes/No Answers

Write a "yes" or "no" short answer after the question.

1. Does Simon work at the International Center? **Yes, he does.**

2. Do Elena and Jorge speak Chinese? **No, they don't.**

3. Do you like coffee? **Yes,** _____

4. Does Ming work in a pharmacy? **No,** _____

5. Do I watch TV every day? **No,** _____

6. Does the dog sleep on the sofa? **Yes,** _____

7. Does Jorge go to the supermarket with Elena?
   Yes, _____

8. Do you buy stamps at the post office? **Yes,** _____

9. Do your friends visit you? **No,** _____

10. Do I write the answers to the questions? **Yes,** _____

G. Short Answers

Circle the correct answer.

1. Who asks Simon about the supermarket? Ming does.

   (Elena does.)

2. Where is the ATM? Near the supermarket.

   Near the post office.

3. Who takes the bus to the post office? Jorge does.

   Sasha does.

4. How far does Elena walk? Four blocks.

   Two blocks.

5. Who goes on tour with the students? Simon does.

   Raquel does.

6. Who writes the answers in the book? I do.

   Elena does.

7. How much does the bus cost? It costs $1.50.

   It costs $2.50.

8. How many stops does Jorge go?   Six stops.

                                     Four stops.

9. Where is the post office?   Near the bank.

                                     Near the pharmacy.

10. Who works in a restaurant?   Ming does.

                                     Raquel does.

H. Questions

Who?   Where?

How Much?   How many?

*Write **Who, Where, How much,** or **How many** in the question.*

1. _____**Where**_____ is the movie theater? —On the corner.

2. _____ are the stores? —They're over there.

3. _____ gives directions? —Simon does.

4. _____ is a subway token? —It's $2.00.

5 _____ goes to work by bus? —Jorge does.

6 _____ stops do you go? —Only two stops.

7. _____ is an airmail stamp? —It's $1.00.

8. _____ paints houses? —Sasha does.

9. _____ blocks do you walk? —Eight blocks.

10. _____ do you live? —Across the street.

I. Plurals

a stamp stamps

a letter  letters

Give the plurals.

	Singular (=1)	Plural (>1)
1.	bank	**banks**
2.	block	
3.	letter	
4.	map	
5.	stop	
6.	train	

J. There is... /There are...

There is	a token machine in the subway. a bus stop on the corner. a hospital over there.
There are	tokens in the machine. people on the bus. visitors in the hospital.

*Write **There is** or **There are** in the sentences.*

1. **There are** _____ many people on the train.

2. **There is** _____ a real estate office over there.

3. _____ a movie theater on the corner.

4. _____ some letters in the mailbox.

5. _____ many cars on the street.

6. _____ a supermarket two blocks away.

K. Prepositions of Place: In/On/At

in   on   at

in	the supermarket / the city / New York
on	the wall / the corner / Main Street / the bus / the train
at	the desk / the bus stop / 715 Maple Avenue

Circle the correct preposition.

1. The information desk is **on** / (**in**) the International Center.

2. Simon is **at** / **on** the information desk.

3. The map is **on** / **at** the wall.

4. Jorge is standing **in** / **at** the map.

5. The ATM is **at** / **in** the supermarket.

6. The food is **in** / **on** the supermarket.

7. The stamps are **in** / **on** the letter.

8. The mailbox is **on** / **in** the corner.

9. The bus is **in** / **at** the bus stop.

10. The convenience store is **on** / **in** Oak Street.

L. Dialogue

Read the dialogue and write the missing words.

ELENA: Jorge, are you going to the _____**post**_____ office?
1. (post/tax)

JORGE: Yes, I'm taking the _____ .
2. (car/bus)

ELENA: _____ is the bus stop?
3. (Who/Where)

JORGE: Near the International _____ .
4. (Center/market)

ELENA: Oh, _____ going there, too. I have to
5. (she's/I'm)

ask Simon about the _____ .
6. (bank/supermarket)

JORGE: Are _____ ready?
7. (they/you)

ELENA: Yes, _____ you?
8. (are/is)

JORGE: Yes, I _____ . Let's _____
9. (am/are)   10. (talk/go)
together.

ELENA: Okay. Let's go.

M. Real People... Real Language

1. Is there a movie theater near your house?

Write the numbers you hear.

a. _____ minute walk, _____ blocks...

b. No movie theater...

c. _____ miles away.

d. A _____ minute drive.

2. Is there a convenience store near your house?

Write the numbers you hear.

a. _____ minute walk away.

b. _____ blocks away.

c. _____ block away.

d. Across the street.

e. _____ block away.

3. Is there a pharmacy near your house?

Do they walk or drive?

a. _____✔_____ walk _____ drive

b. _____ walk _____ drive

c. _____ walk _____ drive

d. _____ walk _____ drive

e. _____ walk _____ drive

VIDEO TRANSCRIPT

Watch and Listen

Simon: Today I'm volunteering at the information desk at the International Center. People usually ask me for directions. Why don't you come and join me?...Hi, Elena! What can I do for you today?

Elena: Can you tell me where the supermarket is?

Simon: It's not far from here.

Elena: Oh, that's good.

Simon: You go outside, you turn left.

Elena: Yes...

Simon: You walk down the street two blocks.

Elena: Two blocks...

Simon: Then you cross the street, and it's right there on the corner.

Elena: That's really near. Is there an ATM there?

Simon: Yes, it's right out front. Here, you can use this map if you like.

Elena: Thanks a lot.

Simon: You're most welcome.

Elena: Go outside and turn left, walk two blocks, cross the street, and the supermarket is on the corner. That's really near.

Simon: Hey, Jorge! Elena just went to the supermarket.

Jorge: Yes. We have a lot of things to do today. Is there a post office around here?

Simon: There's a mailbox down the street.

Jorge: No, but I need to buy some stamps.

Simon: In that case, you'll have to take a bus to the post office.

Jorge: Where's the bus stop?

Simon: Go outside, turn right, and it's at the end of the block.

Jorge: How much does it cost?

Simon: $1.50 in exact change.

Jorge: And how many stops do I go?

Simon: I think it's about four. You get off at the pharmacy.

Jorge: So the post office is near the pharmacy.

Simon: Right, you'll see it when you get there.

Jorge: Thanks, Simon.

Simon: Don't mention it.

Jorge: Go outside, turn right, take the bus at the end of the block, go four stops, and get off at the pharmacy. Got it!

Simon: While Jorge works out my directions, let's review some phrases to help you find your way around town?

To ask where something is, you say:

Where's the movie theater? or

Can you tell me where the hospital is? or

Are there any banks around here?

In response, you might hear:

It's **over there.**   or

It's **right here.**   or

It's **across the street.**

Now let's listen to some people give directions.

Unit 4
Shopping for Food

A. Odd One Out

Cross out the food that is a different color:

1. red: apples / strawberries / ba~~nanas~~ / tomatoes
2. yellow: butter / carrots / bananas
3. white: onions / rice / soup / milk
4. brown: potatoes / juice / bread / eggs
5. orange: carrots / oranges / juice / sauce

B. What is it?

Write the missing letters.

1. Fruit:

   A **P P L E** S

   O _ _ _ _ _ _ S

   B _ _ _ _ _ S

   S _ _ _ _ B _ _ _ _ _ S

2. Vegetables:

   P _ _ _ _ _ _ _ S

   O _ _ _ _ S

   C _ _ _ _ _ S

   T _ _ _ _ _ _ _ S

3. Dairy:

   M _ _ K

   E _ _ S

   B _ _ _ _ R

4. Canned goods: S __ __ P

S __ __ __ E

C. Verbs: Future with *Going To*

I	am going to __	we	are going to __
you	are going to __	you	are going to __
he / she / it	is going to __	they	are going to __

yesterday   today   tomorrow

future:
tomorrow
next week
next month
next year

Write the verbs in the sentences.

1. Raquel, Ming and Elena **are going to go** to the supermarket. (go)

2. Raquel _____ two pounds of apples. (buy)

3. Ming _____ a half gallon of juice. (get)

4. Elena _____ a box of spaghetti. (look for)

5. Later, they _____ lunch at Elena's house. (have)

6. I _____ a movie tonight. (see)

7. You _____ to school tomorrow. (drive)
8. It _____ next week. (snow)
9. We _____ a vacation in July. (take)
10. Jorge _____ a new apartment soon. (rent)

D. Negatives

I	am not going to __	we	are not __
you	are not going to __	you	are not __
he/she/it	is not going to __	they	are going to __

Contractions: I am = I'm; you are = you're; he is = he's
or: are not = aren't; is not = isn't.

Write the subject pronoun and the negative form of the verb.

1. __**They aren't going to**__ go to the movie theater.
(Raquel, Ming, and Elena)

2. _____ get any bananas. (Raquel)

3. _____ buy much juice. (Ming)

4. _____ eat many oranges. (Elena)

5. _____ have pizza for lunch. (they)

6. _____ paint next weekend. (Sasha)

7. _____ take the bus to the
bank. (you)

8. _____ buy any fruit at the
market. (I)

9. _____ drink any milk. (the dog)

10. _____ mail the letters today. (we)

E. Yes/No Answers

Circle the correct answer.

1. Is Raquel going to buy a pint of strawberries? Yes, she is.

    No, she isn't.

2. Is Ming going to get a bunch of bananas? Yes, she is.

    No, she isn't.

3. Is Elena going to buy a bag of potatoes? Yes, she is.

    No, she isn't.

4. Are they going to use coupons at the checkout counter? Yes, they are.

    No, they aren't.

5. Is Jorge going to make lasagna? Yes, he is.

    No, he isn't.

6. Are Sasha and Simon going to eat lunch at Elena's house? Yes, they are.

    No, they aren't.

F. Short Answers

Draw a line from the question to the answer.

1. How many pounds of apples is Raquel going to buy?   a. A five-pound bag.

2. How much are apples?   b. Some tomatoes.

3. What kind of fruit would Ming like?   c. A dozen.

4. How many oranges does Elena need?   d. Two pounds.

5. How many potatoes is Raquel going to get?   e. A few.

6. How much are the onions?   f. A quart.

7. What is Elena going to buy for the salad? g. Orange juice.

8. How many eggs does Raquel need?   h. $1.29 a pound.

9. What kind of juice is Ming going to buy? i. Bananas.

10. How much milk would Elena like?   j. $.99 a pound.

G. Questions

How much?

How many?

*Write **How much** or **How many** in the questions.*

1. ___**How much**___ juice is Ming going to buy?

2. _____ eggs is Raquel going to get?

3. _____ lasagna is Elena going to make?

4. _____ rooms is Sasha going to paint?

5. _____ classes is Simon going to teach?

6. _____ money is Jorge going to make?

7. _____ places are the students going to tour?

8. _____ cookies are you going to eat?

9. _____ milk is the cat going to drink?

10. _____ soup are the children going to eat?

H. Singular/Plural Nouns

Write the plural next to the singular.

	Singular (=1)	Plural (>1)
1.	apple	**apples**
2.	banana	
3.	carrot	
4.	egg	
5.	onion	
6.	potato	**potatoes***
7.	tomato	
8.	strawberry	**strawberries**†
9.	raspberry	
10.	cherry	

* Remember: y → ie before s.   † Remember: after o or u, add es.

I. Money

dollar   quarter   dime   nickel   penny

How much money did they spend?

Raquel	
• apples	$2.58
• potatoes	$1.99
• eggs	$1.39
• bread	$1.59
• soup	$ .99
Total	$8.54
Cash	$10.00
Change	$1.46

• bananas	$ .89
• onions	$ .99
• juice	$1.49
• rice	$2.99
Total	
Cash	$10.00
Change	

• oranges	$2.99
• tomatoes	$2.49
• milk	$1.79
• spaghetti	$ .85
• tomato sauce	$1.09
Total	
Cash	$10.00
Change	

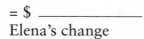

= $ _____
Raquel's change

= $ _____
Elena's change

= $ _____
Ming's change

....

J. Count and Noncount Nouns

How many?   How much?

a	tomato	_____	rice
some a few a lot of many	tomatoes	some a little a lot of much	rice
no not many	tomatoes	no not much	rice

Write the food from Raquel's, Ming's, and Elena's lists.

1. some / a few / a lot / many:

     apples

     potatoes

     eggs

_____

_____

_____

2. some / a little / a lot of / much:

     bread

     soup

_____

_____

_____

K. Recipe: Jorge's Tacos

Unscramble the words in Jorge's recipe.

a pound of ground **BEEF**   **SALT**   , pepper, spices
                  FEBE   LAST
some _____   a little grated _____
       CLUTEET   HEESEEC
a _____   a jar of _____
       TOOTAM   LASAS
a few _____ shells   a pint of sour _____
       COAT   RAMEC

- Cook the ground beef in a frying pan with salt, pepper, and spices.
- Cut the lettuce and tomato.
- Warm the taco shells in the oven.
- When the ground beef is done, put it in the taco.
- Put the cheese, sour cream, and salsa on top.
- Add the lettuce and tomato.
- Enjoy your taco!

L. Dialogue

SIMON: Do _____ ever cook, Jorge?
        1. (you/he)

JORGE: Of course. I'm going to _____ tonight.
                               2. (wash/cook)

SIMON: Oh, really? _____ are you going to make?
                   3. (Who / What)

JORGE: Something easy, like _____.
                            4. (lasagna/tacos)

SIMON: What do you _____ to make tacos?
                   5. (need/eat)

JORGE: You need taco shells, ground beef, lettuce, tomatoes,

        _____, and salsa.
        6. (milk/cheese)

SIMON: And _____ you have all those things?
           7. (do / are)

JORGE: I have everything except the salsa. I need to get

        _____.
        8. (any/some)

SIMON: I'd like to try making tacos _____.
                                    9. (tonight/next year)

JORGE: If you _____ help, just call me.
              10. (need/have)

SIMON: Okay. I want to surprise Raquel with

_____ tonight.
        11. (breakfast/dinner)

JORGE: If I see _____ , I won't say anything.
                        12. (her/him)

M. Containers

Can you think of any more?

1. **a bag of**
   oranges
   potatoes
   onions
   _____

2. **a bottle of**
   ketchup
   wine
   milk
   soy sauce
   _____

3. **a box of**
   spaghetti
   noodles
   cake mix
   _____

4. **a bunch of**
   grapes
   carrots
   bananas
   _____

5. **a can of**
   soup
   tomato sauce
   peas
   pineapple
   _____

6. **a carton of**
   juice
   milk
   eggnog
   _____

7. **a head of**
   lettuce
   cabbage
   garlic
   _____

8. **a jar of**
   jelly
   peanut butter
   pickles
   olives
   _____

9. **a roll of**
   toilet paper
   paper towel
   film

   _____
   _____

10. **a tube of**
    toothpaste
    shaving cream
    bath gel

    _____
    _____

Now write your shopping list here.

_____   _____
_____   _____
_____   _____
_____   _____
_____   _____
_____   _____
_____   _____

N. Real People...Real Language

1. How often do you go food shopping?

Underline the word they say.

a. Once or twice a week/ **month**

b. Once a week/month

c. Never/hardly ever

d. Once every two/three weeks

2. What do you buy?

Cross out the food they don't buy.

a. fruit / sandwich meat / ch~~ee~~se / butter / meat / vegetables

b. canned goods / eggs / fruits / vegetables / juices

c. bread / meat / cheese / rice / vegetables

3. What's your favorite dish and what's in it?

Write the missing word in the recipe.

a. Pizza: crust, sauce, **onions**, mushrooms, peppers

b. Sancocho: chicken, beef, yams, potatoes, _____ , plantains

c. Arroz con pollo: chicken, _____ , peas, tomatoes, onions, spices

d. Lubyeh: lamb, string beans, tomato _____

4. Do you do all your food shopping in one store?

Put a check by the number.

a. _____ 1 ✔ 2 _____ 3

b. _____ 1 _____ 2 _____ 3

c. _____ 1 _____ 2 _____ 3

5. How much do you spend on food each week?

Underline the money they spend.

a. <u>$80 to $100</u> / $100 to $180 every two weeks

b. $50 / $150 a week

c. $50 / $150 a week

d. $100 / $200 a week

VIDEO TRANSCRIPT

Watch and Listen

Raquel: Elena, Ming, and I are going shopping for food. Why don't you join us?

Ming: Raquel, what are you going to get?

Raquel: I need some apples. How much are they?

Elena: These are $1.29 a pound.

Raquel: I'm going to get two pounds.

Ming: I think I prefer bananas.

Elena: And I'm going to get some oranges.

Raquel: How about the vegetables? I need a five-pound bag of potatoes.

Ming: Onions are on sale—only $.99.

Elena: Jorge loves salad. I'm going to get lots of tomatoes.

Raquel: Ming, can you hand me a dozen eggs?

Ming: I'd like a little juice.

Elena: Could I have a quart of milk? A box a spaghetti and a jar of tomato sauce... (*Looking at their lists*)

Ming: Some rice...

Raquel: A loaf of bread and a can of soup...

Raquel: You know what? Shopping makes me hungry. How about lunch?

Elena: Come to my house. I'm going to make lasagna.

Raquel: That sounds great, Elena!

Ming: But only if you let us help you.

Raquel: While we're having lunch, here are a few useful phrases to remember when you go shopping.

When you need something, you can say:

        I need some bread and milk.   or

        She'd like a pound of cheese.   or

        Can we have a few apples?

When you need to do something, you say:

> **You need to** go shopping. or
>
> **He'd like to** eat some grapes. or
>
> **They have to** buy some rice.

Another thing to remember when you go shopping for food is that you can save money if you use coupons at the check out counter. Now, let's listen to some other people talk about going shopping.

Unit 5
Finding an Apartment

A. Odd One Out

Cross out the furniture or furnishing that is not in each room.

table
chairs
stove
refrigerator
~~bed~~
sink

1. KITCHEN   dishwasher

sofa
coffee table
lamp
rocking chair
stereo
TV

2. LIVING ROOM   shower

bed
dresser
mirror
night table
desk
chair
closet

3. BEDROOM   oven

sink
toilet
microwave
bathtub

4. BATHROOM   cabinet

B. Verbs: Present Tense—*Can/Can't*

He **can lift** the suitcase.   She **can't lift** the suitcase.

I	can / can't	we	can / can't
you	can / can't	you	can / can't
he/she/it	can / can't	they	can / can't

Contraction: cannot = **can't**

yesterday	today	tomorrow
	PRESENT	

*Write **can** or **can't** in the sentences.*

1. Simon _____ **can** _____ speak English.

2. He _____ **can't** _____ speak Russian.

3. Sasha _____ paint houses.

4. He _____ do social work.

5. Ming _____ paint houses.

6. She _____ cook Chinese food.

Questions: Can Jorge cook Chinese food?   No, he can't.

*Write **Can** in the questions. Write "yes" or "no" short answers.*

7. ____**Can**____ Jorge cook Chinese food?   **No, he can't.**

8. _____ he cook Mexican food?   _____

9. _____ Elena work as a cashier?   _____

10. _____ she work as an engineer?   _____

C. Verbs: Past Tense—Could/Couldn't

I	could / couldn't	we	could / couldn't
you	could / couldn't	you	could / couldn't
he / she / it	could / couldn't	they	could / couldn't

yesterday   today   tomorrow

past

*Write **could** or **couldn't** in the sentences.*

1. Last Sunday, Simon ____**could**____ find some cheap apartments in the newspaper.

2. Jorge ____**couldn't**____ rent an expensive apartment.

3. The real estate agent _____ show them three apartments.

4. Jorge _____ choose an apartment without Elena.

5. Elena _____ see the apartments on Monday.

6. They _____ rent the apartment on Beals Boulevard.

Questions: Could Jorge and Elena buy a pet?   No, they couldn't.

*Write **could** in the questions. Write "yes" or "no" short answers.*

7. ___**Could**___ they have a pet in their new apartment?
   No, they couldn't.

8. _____ Simon and Raquel help them move in?
   Yes, _____

9. _____ Sasha help them paint their apartment?
   Yes, _____

10. _____ Ming help them move?
    No, _____

D. *Can/Can't or Could/Couldn't*

Circle the correct verb in the sentence.

1. I can / can't speak English well.

2. Simon could / couldn't go to the real estate office with Jorge.

3. Jorge and Elena could / couldn't find an apartment with parking and laundry.

4. Raquel can / can't speak Chinese.

5. Ming could / couldn't help paint the apartment.

6. Elena can / can't make lasagna.

7. She could / couldn't have a cat or a dog in the new apartment.

8. Sasha could / couldn't paint his friend's apartment.

E. Short Answers

Write a short answer after the question.

1. Can you speak Russian? **Yes, I can.**
2. Could Jorge speak English ten years ago? **No, he couldn't.**
3. Can dogs run fast? **Yes,**
4. Could Raquel go shopping with Ming and Elena?
   Yes,
5. Can you understand the video? **Yes,**
6. Could Jorge pay for the apartment on Owens Avenue?
   No,
7. Can we use coupons at the check out counter?
   Yes,
8. Could you write in English last year? **No,**
9. Can they find a job in the classified ads? **No,**
10. Could Ming go on the tour with Raquel and Sasha?
    Yes,

F. Adjectives: Opposites

cheap	≠	expensive
easy	≠	difficult
fast	≠	slow
funny	≠	serious
interesting	≠	boring
large/big	≠	small/little
light	≠	heavy
new	≠	old
pretty	≠	ugly
same	≠	different
short	≠	tall

Circle the words that are correct.

1. The apartment on Owens Avenue is...

   (new)   ugly   (large)   (expensive)

2. The apartment on Stanford Street is...

   old   small   pretty   different

3. The apartment on Beals Boulevard is...

   large   cheap   interesting   old

G. Adjectives: Comparative and Superlative

Superlative	Comparative	Adjective	Comparative	Superlative
-est	-er		-er	-est
least	less		more	most

Use the **comparative** when comparing **two** things or people.
Use the **superlative** when comparing **three or more** things or people.

Jorge is taller than Ming.   Sasha is taller than Jorge.

Sasha is tallest of the three.

Fill in the chart with the comparative and superlative forms.

	ADJECTIVE	COMPARATIVE (+/-)	SUPERLATIVE (+++/- - -)
1.	large*	larger*	largest*
2.	small	smaller	smallest
3.	new		
4.	old		
5.	heavy†	heavier	heaviest
6.	pretty†		
7.	easy†		
8.	expensive $$	more expensive $$$	most expensive $$$$
9.	interesting		
10.	difficult $E = mc^2$	less difficult $2x + y = 7$	least difficult $2 \times 3 = 6$
11.	serious		

*e + er = er; e+est = est † y + er = ier; y + est = iest

....

H. More Comparatives and Superlatives

Jorge looked at these three apartments:

- **Owens Avenue:** $950   new   large   modern
- **Stanford Street:** $900   old   small   nice
- **Beals Boulevard:** $850   old   large   interesting

Write the comparative or superlative in the sentences.

1. The apartment on Stanford Street is _____**older**_____
   than the one*on Owens Avenue. (old)

2. The one on Owens Avenue is _____ than the one on Stanford Street. (new)

3. The one on Beals Boulevard is _____ than the one on Stanford Street. (large)

4. The one on Owens Avenue is **more expensive** than the one on Beals Boulevard. (expensive)

5. The one on Beals Boulevard is _____ than the one on Owens Avenue. (interesting)

6. The one on Owens Avenue is _____ than the one on Stanford Street. (modern)

7. The one on Owens Avenue is the **newest** of the three. (new)

8. The one on Beals Boulevard is the _____ of the three. (cheap)

9. The one on Owens Avenue is the **most expensive** of the three. (expensive)

10. The one on Beals Boulevard is the _____ of the three. (interesting)

*one = apartment

I. Questions: Which/Which one

The **apartment** on Owens Avenue is new.
The **one** on Beals Boulevard is old.

Which apartment is the most expensive?
The **one** on Owens Avenue.

Which one is the least expensive?
The **one** on Beals Boulevard.

*Write **Which** or **Which one** in the question.*

1. _____**Which**_____ apartment is the most expensive?
2. ____**Which one**____ is the cheapest?
3. _____ house is more interesting?
4. _____ is older?
5. _____ sofa is the newest?
6. _____ is the largest?
7. _____ is the heaviest?
8. _____ car is faster?
9. _____ is prettier?
10. _____ is easier to drive?

J. Dialogue

Read the dialogue and write the missing words.

JORGE: Elena! Simon, and I found a ____**nice**____ apartment!
1. (nice/ugly)

ELENA: Oh, really? _____ is it?
2. (What/Where)

JORGE: It's _____ the International Center on Beals
3. (near / far)
Boulevard.

ELENA: That's a great location. How _____ is it?
4. (much/many)

JORGE: It's not too _____—$850 a month.
5. (large/expensive)

ELENA: How _____ bedrooms?
6. (much/ many)

JORGE: It has a _____ one and a small one. Or one
7. (large/cheap)
could be an office.

ELENA: Sounds great! When _____ I see it?
8. (can/can't)

JORGE: Anytime _____ want.
9. (she/you)

ELENA: Let's make an appointment for _____.
10. (yesterday / tomorrow)

JORGE: Okay. I think you're going to _____ it.
11. (like / buy)

ELENA: I _____ wait to see it!
12. (can / can't)

K. Newspapers: Classified Ads

Look at these classified ads and fill in the chart.

Apt. 1: 1 bdrm. w/prking, lndry, h+hw included. Only $800/mo. Deposit req. Call 555-6734 eve.

Apt. 3: 2 bdrm w/2 bthrm, h+hw, A/C, dish.+disp, wash+dryer, gar., $1,200/mo. Call 555-4000 days.

Apt. 2: 3 bdrms, 1 1/2 bthrm, h+hw, only $1,500. Call mgr. at 555-4872.

Apt. 4: 4 bdrm, 2 bthrm, 2 pking sp. A/C, lndry, h+hw, $2,000. 555-1032

	APT. 1	APT. 2	APT. 3	APT. 4
Bedrooms	**1**			
Bathrooms	**1**			
Parking	**Yes**			
Laundry	**Yes**			
Heat & hot water	**Yes**			
Rent/month	**$800**			

L. Real People...Real Language

1. What part of the city do you live in?

Check the words you hear.

a. ✔——— Mission Hill   ———— Mission Hall

b. ———— Hyde Pub   ———— Hyde Park

c. ———— West Roxbury   ———— East Roxbury

d. ———— South Cambridge   ———— North Cambridge

2. How did you find your apartment?

Circle the words you hear.

a. Through a friend / (realtor.)

b. Through a friend / realtor.

c. Through my doctor / dentist.

d. Walking / driving up and down the streets.

e. Through a real estate agent / newspaper.

3. What is your apartment or house like?

Circle the number of bedrooms.

a.   1   (2)   3   4

b.   1   2   3   4

c.   1   2   3   4

d.   1   2   3   4

e.   1   2   3   4

4. Is your rent very high?

Check the numbers you hear.

a. ✔——— $575   ———— $757

b. ———— $300   ———— $600

c. ———— $2,500   ———— $1,500

d. _____ low   _____ high

e. _____ $400   _____ $800

5. Would you like to move to a different area?

Circle the answer you hear.

a.   (yes)   no

b.   yes   no

c.   yes   no

d.   yes   no

e.   yes   no

VIDEO TRANSCRIPT

Watch and Listen

Simon: Do you see any apartments you like, Jorge?

Jorge: A few.

Simon: Where are they?

Jorge: Not far from here.

Simon: Are they expensive?

Jorge: Well, the two-bedrooms are expensive, but the one-bedrooms are cheaper.

Simon: Which would you like?

Jorge: We'd like a two-bedroom, but we can also take a one-bedroom.

Simon: Let's call and ask to see them.

Jorge: Okay, can I use the phone here?

Simon: Go right ahead.

Jorge: Yes. Hi, I'm interested in a few of the apartments listed in the paper... This afternoon would be great.... Two o'clock? Perfect...My name is Jorge Gonzalez...Okay. See you at two. Thank you.

At the real estate office.

Jorge: Hi. I have an appointment at two.

Simon: We'd like to look at some apartments.

Agent: You must be Jorge. Come in. Sit down. So, what are you looking for?

Jorge: A one- or two-bedroom, not too expensive, with laundry and parking.

Agent: No problem. Let's see... There are three apartments I could show you: on Stanford Street, on Owens Avenue, and on Beals Boulevard.

Jorge: How much is the rent?

Agent: They're all under $1,000—with heat and hot water included.

Simon: Could you tell us more about them?

Agent: The one on Owens Avenue is brand new.

Jorge: What about the one on Stanford Street?

Agent: It's nice, but it's old.

Jorge: And the one on Beals Boulevard?

Agent: It's pretty big and not too expensive.

Simon: Why don't we look at that one first?

Agent: All right. Come fill out an application, and I'll get the keys.

Simon: While Jorge is filling out an application, here are some phrases to remember.

When making a request, you say:

Can I use the phone?   or

Could we see some apartments today?   or

Can you show us the kitchen?   or

Could you tell us the address?

When suggesting something, you say:

Let's call and make an appointment.   or

Let's take the subway to the agency.   or

Why don't we look at the big one first?   or

Why don't you sign the contract tomorrow?

Now let's listen to people talk about their apartments.

Unit 6
Opening a Bank Account

A. Vocabulary Practice

Write the letters in the words.

1. SAVE: __sav__ ings account

   to __save__ money

2. CARD: ATM _____

   credit _____

3. CHECK: _____ ing account

   pay _____

   travelers _____ s

Fill in the vowels.

4. put into your account

D <u>E</u> P <u>O</u> S <u>I</u> T

5. take out of your account

W __ T H D R __ W

6. bank worker

T __ L L __ R

7. money in bills and coins

C __ S H

B. Verbs: Future with *Will/Won't*

I	will / won't	we	will / won't
you	will / won't	you	will / won't
he / she / it	will / won't	they	will / won't

Contractions: will not = won't

yesterday   today   tomorrow

future:
tomorrow
next
week/month/year
in a week/month/year

*Write **will** or **won't** in the sentences.*

1. Jorge and Elena _____**will**_____ deposit $1,000 today.

2. They _____**won't**_____ pay a fee if their balance is $1,500.

3. The bank _____ send their ATM cards next week.

4. They _____ get their checks next week, too.

5. Jorge's company _____ deposit his paycheck directly.

6. They _____ apply for a credit card today.

7. The bank teller _____ take care of their application.

8. They _____ send money back to Mexico.

9. They _____ buy a car now.

10. The bank _____ lend them money to buy the car.

C. Yes/No Answers

Write a "yes" or "no" short answer after the question.

1. Will Jorge and Elena open individual accounts?
   No, they won't.

2. Will they open a joint account? **Yes, they will.**
3. Will they both deposit money? **Yes,** _____
4. Will they use the ATM? **Yes,** _____
5. Will they buy a car this month? **No,** _____
6. Will you buy a car in a few months? **Yes,** _____
7. Will the weather be nice tomorrow? **No,** _____
8. Will we go to the supermarket next week? **Yes,** _____
9. Will the bank give you traveler's checks? **Yes,** _____
10. Will you get a credit card next year? **No,** _____

D. Questions

Draw a line from the question to the answer.

1. What will Jorge and Elena do today?   a. A bank teller.
2. Who will they speak with?   b. A joint account.
3. What kind of account will they open?   c. A thousand dollars.
4. How much will they deposit today?   d. By wire transfer.
5. When will their checks arrive?   e. In a few months.
6. Will they apply for a credit card today?   f. Next week.
7. How will they send money to Mexico?   g. No, they won't.
8. Why will they apply for a loan?   h. Open a bank account.
9. Will they apply for the loan today?   i. To buy a car.
10. When will they buy a car?   j. Yes, they will.

E. Questions: How often?

*Write **How often** in the questions.*

1. _____**How often**_____ can people use the ATM? —Every day.

2. _____ does Raquel see Ming at the International Center? —Every Wednesday.

3. _____ does Sasha deposit his paycheck? —Once a week.*

4. _____ does Simon withdraw his money? —On Monday and Friday.

5. _____ do Jorge and Elena receive a bank statement? —Every month.

6. _____ does it snow in Russia? —Every winter.

7. _____ does it snow in the Dominican Republic? —Never.

8. _____ does it rain in your city? —A few days a month.

*once a week = one time a week; twice a week = two times a week

F. Adverbs of Frequency

100%	always	Elena *always* goes to the supermarket on Saturday.
80%	usually	Sasha *usually* paints apartments.
60%	often	Raquel *often* cooks dinner in the evening.
40%	sometimes	Jorge *sometimes* cooks dinner for Elena.
20%	rarely	Simon *rarely* cooks dinner for Raquel.
0%	never	Ming *never* works in the restaurant on Sunday.

1. People can ___**always**___ use the ATM. (every day)

2. The bank is ___**usually**___ open from 8:00 A.M. to 4:00 P.M. (Monday to Friday, Saturdays 9:00 to 3:00)

3. Sasha _____ deposits his paycheck into his account on Friday. (every Friday)

4. Banks _____ approve credit card applications. (4 out of 10 times)

5. It _____ snows in Russia in winter. (0° – 40° F.)

6. It _____ snows in the Dominican Republic. (70° – 90°F.)

7. Sasha _____ works on Sunday. (three times a year)

8. Simon _____ walks to the International Center. (four times a week)

9. Jorge and Elena _____ speak Spanish with each other. (not always)

10. They _____ speak English with Simon.

G. *Too* and *Enough*

A car is **too expensive.**   They don't have **enough money.**

*Write **too** or **enough** in the sentences.*

1. Can Jorge and Elena buy a car now?

   —No, they can't. A car is ___**too**___ expensive.

2. Can Elena make lasagna?

   —Yes, she can. She has _____ **enough** _____ tomato sauce.

3. Can Simon make chicken curry?

   —No, he can't. It's _____ difficult.

4. Can Ming go to the supermarket today?

   —Yes, she can. She has _____ time.

5. Can Ming lift a refrigerator?

   —No, she can't. It's _____ heavy.

6. Can Sasha paint houses?

   —Yes, he can. He has _____ experience.

7. Can Sasha wear Jorge's shoes?

   —No, he can't. They're _____ small.

8. Can Jorge wear Sasha's shoes?

   —No, he can't. They're _____ big.

9. Can Simon teach high school English?

   —Yes, he can. He has _____ education.

10. Can Jorge and Elena rent an apartment?

   —Yes, they can. They have _____ money.

H. Object Pronouns

<u>Simon</u> takes <u>Jorge and Elena</u> to the bank.
subject   object

<u>He</u> takes <u>them</u> to the bank.
subject   object

SUBJECT	OBJECT	SUBJECT	OBJECT
I	me	we	us
you	you	you	you
he	him		
she	her	they	them
it	it		

Write the sentence using an object pronoun.

1. Simon will meet <u>Raquel</u> at the center.
   Simon will meet her at the center.

2. Jorge and Elena will ask <u>Sasha</u> to paint their new apartment.

   _____

3. The bank teller will mail <u>a loan application</u> to Jorge and Elena.

   _____

4. Ming will serve <u>people</u> in the restaurant.

   _____

5. Raquel will take <u>the book</u> to the library.

   _____

6. Simon gives <u>his students</u> homework every day.

   _____

7. You can get <u>cash</u> from the ATM.

   _____

8. Jorge can teach <u>Simon</u> to cook.

   _____

9. Elena can show <u>Ming</u> her new apartment.

   _____

10. Sasha can take <u>a sandwich</u> to work.

   _____

I. If Clauses: Bank Advice

If it rains, you'll get wet.

If you take your umbrella, you won't get wet.

Write the missing word.

1. If you go to the bank, you can get an 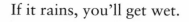 .
   (apple/application)

2. If you are married, you can open a _____ account.
   (joint/individual)

3. If you deposit money, your _____ will go up.
   (deposit/balance)

4. If you withdraw money, your _____ will go down.
   (balance/paycheck)

5. If the bank is closed, you can use the _____ .
   (ATM/teller)

6. If you save money, your _____ will grow.
   (savings account/bills)

7. If you have an account, you can apply for a _____ card.
   (credit/loan)

8. If you're going on a trip, you can get traveler's _____ .
   (cards/checks)

9. If you're going to buy a car, you can ask for a _____ .
   (loan/ fee)

10. If you get a loan, you will have to pay _____ .
    (fees/interest)

J. A Bank Statement

Look at Jorge and Elena's bank statement and answer the questions.

Jorge and Elena Gonzalez					Checking Account
1735 Beals Boulevard					Account Number: 407238
Center City, USA					

Date	Check No.	Description	Deductions (-)	Additions (+)	Balance
11-01		Starting Balance			1,000.00
11-01	0001	Beals Blvd. Mgmt.	850.00		150.00
11-01		Deposit		1,500.00	1,650.00
11-05	0002	City Electric	36.64		1,613.36
11-07	0003	City Telephone	68.12		1,545.24
11-10	0004	Super Shop	29.67		1,515.57
11-12		Withdrawal ATM	50.00		1,465.57
11-15	0005	City Gas	12.74		1,452.83
11-20	0006	Best Dressed	29.99		1,422.84
11-25		Withdrawal ATM	50.00		1,372.84
11-31		Ending Balance			1,372.84

1. Check 0001 is for rent. How much is it? _____ **$850** _____

2. When does Jorge deposit his paycheck of $1,500? _____

3. How much is the telephone bill? _____

4. How many ATM withdrawals are there? _____

5. What is the ending balance? _____

K. Conjunctions: And Versus Or

• Jorge and Elena are opening a checking and a savings account.

• You can pay by check or credit card.

• They do **not** allow dogs **or** cats in the apartment building.

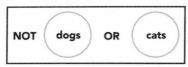

*Write **and** or **or** in the sentences.*

1. Jorge and Elena pay for electricity, gas, ___**and**___ telephone.

2. They don't pay for water _____ parking.

3. Jorge can take a bus _____ a train to work.

4. Ming works at the restaurant on Monday, Wednesday, _____ Friday.

5. Simon likes Dominican _____ American food.

6. Will Simon make spaghetti _____ tacos?

L. Conjunctions: *And* Versus *But*

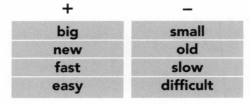

+	−
big	small
new	old
fast	slow
easy	difficult

BUT: (+/−)   or   (−/+)   AND: (+/+)   or   (−/−)

The apartment on Owens Avenue is new and big. (+/+)

The apartment on Beals Boulevard is big but old. (+/-)

The apartment on Stanford Street is old but nice. (-/+)

*Write **and** or **but** in the sentences.*

1. The apartment on Stanford Street is big __**but**__ old.

2. Using the ATM is fast _____ easy.

3. Jorge and Elena are going to apply for a credit card, _____ not for a loan.

4. A wire transfer is fast _____ secure.

5. Today is cold _____ sunny.

6. Ming works on weekdays _____ not on weekends.

M. Real People...Real Language

1. Where is your bank account?

Circle the bank you hear.

a.	(BankBoston)	Fleet Bank	U.S. Trust
b.	BankBoston	Fleet Bank	U.S. Trust
c.	BankBoston	Fleet Bank	U.S. Trust
d.	BankBoston	Fleet Bank	U.S. Trust
e.	BankBoston	Fleet Bank	U.S. Trust

2. Do you prefer big banks or small banks?

Check the one you hear.

a. __✔__ big _____ small

b. _____ big _____ small

c. —— big   —— small

d. —— big   —— small

e. —— big   —— small

f. —— big   —— small

g. —— big   —— small

3. What services do you use at the bank?

Put a ✔ under the ones you hear.

	CHECKING	SAVINGS	ATM
a.	✔		
b.			
c.			
d.			

4. How often do you use the ATM?

Draw a line to the correct phrase.

a.   not often

b.   3 or 4 times a week

c.   a lot

d.   twice a week

5. Which do you use more often: checks or credit cards?

Draw a box around the words you hear.

a.   checks   [credit cards]

b.   checks   credit cards

c.   checks   credit cards

d.   checks   credit cards

e.	checks	credit cards
f.	checks	credit cards
g.	checks	credit cards
h.	checks	credit cards

Video Transcript

Watch and Listen

Ms. Lee: So, what can I do for you today?

Jorge: We'd like to open a bank account.

Ms. Lee: Individual accounts or a joint account?

Elena: A joint one is better.

Ms. Lee: Yes, and you can get both checking and savings.

Jorge: Do we have to pay a service fee?

Ms. Lee: If you have a minimum balance of $1,500, there are no fees.

Elena: I hope we can do that.

Jorge: Don't worry; we both work.

Ms. Lee: Okay. How much would you like to deposit now?

Jorge: $1,000 now and more next week.

Ms. Lee: Good. You'll get a statement with your balance every month.

Elena: And when do we get our checks and ATM cards?

Ms. Lee: You'll get temporary checks now and permanent checks and your ATM cards in about a week.

Jorge: So, we deposit our paychecks at the teller's window, right?

Elena: Or ATM.

Ms. Lee: Yes, and some companies offer direct deposit, so your paycheck can be deposited into your account automatically.

Jorge: So, no waiting in line!

Ms. Lee: That's right... Any other questions?

Elena: Can we have a credit card application, too?

Ms. Lee: Sure. You can fill it out at home and bring it in later.

Elena: How do we send money home to our families in Mexico?

Ms. Lee: You can do that by money order or wire transfer.

Jorge: We're also thinking about buying a car. Do you think we can get a loan?

Ms. Lee: It depends on how much you want to borrow and how much you earn. Would you like to fill out a application?

Jorge: Let's come back and talk about it in a few months.

Elena: Good idea.

Ms. Lee: Thank you for banking with us. See you again soon.

Jorge: Thank you. Good-bye.

Elena: Good-bye.

Simon: That wasn't too difficult, was it? Let's go over some phrases you'll need at the bank.

When someone in a bank or store sees you, they might say:

> **How may I help you?**   or
>
> **What can I do for you today?**

You can reply like this:

> **I'd like** some traveler's checks.   or
>
> **We'd like to** apply for a loan.

To show ownership, you say:

> **You have** a new credit card.   or
>
> **She has** a checking account here.

To show that something is necessary, you say:

> **You have to** mail your payment on time.   or
>
> **She has to** open a savings account.

Now let's listen to people talk about different bank services.

Unit 7
Using the Telephone

A. Vocabulary Practice

Write the words in the sentences.

1. When the telephone rings, you **p i c k** it up.
2. When the telephone is busy, you **h** _ _ _ up.
3. When you aren't home, the answering machine takes
   a **m** _ _ _ _ _ _ .
4. When you dial a number, the phone **r** _ _ _ _ .
5. When you call the **o** _ _ _ _ _ _ _ _ , she gives you
   information.
6. You can buy a **p** _ _ _ _ **c** _ _ _ at a store.
7. You can dial a **t** _ _ _ _ - **f** _ _ _ _ number without
   paying.
8. You have to go to the airport to take a **f** _ _ _ _ _ _ .
9. You have to call the airlines to check the plane
   s _ _ _ _ _ _ _ _ .
10. You pay less for a round-trip ticket than two **o** _ _ - **w** _ _
    tickets.

B. Verbs: Simple Past—Regular

_____ + ed

I	work**ed**	we	work**ed**
you	work**ed**	you	work**ed**
he/she/it	work**ed**	they	work**ed**

yesterday   today   tomorrow

past:
yesterday
last week/month/year
a long time ago
in 1960

Write the verbs in the past tense.

1. want ___**wanted**___

2. look _____

3. dial _____

4. ask _____

5. call _____

6. receive* _____

7. pick _____

8. press _____

9. listen _____

10. offer _____

*e + ed = ed

Now write the verbs in the sentences.

1. Ming ___**wanted**___ to go to her sister's wedding.

2. Raquel _____ in the newspaper for cheap flights.

3. Ming _____ 1-800-555-TOUR.

4. She _____ about ticket prices to Hong Kong.

5. Sasha's friends _____ from Russia.

6. They _____ their visas to come to the U.S.

7. Sasha _____ up the phone to make a call.

8. He _____ the buttons for train schedules.

9. He _____ to the information.

10. Then he _____ to put up Ming's bookshelves.

C. Negatives

I	did not work	we	did not work
you	did not work	you	did not work
he/she/it	did not work	they	did not work

Contraction: did not = didn't

Write the subject pronoun and the negative form of the verbs in Exercise B.

1. **She didn't want** to go to her cousin's wedding.

2. _____ in the newspaper for expensive flights.

3. _____ 1-800-666-TOUR.

4. _____ about ticket prices to Russia.

5. _____ from Mexico.

6. _____ their visas to come to Canada.

7. _____ up the newspaper to make a call.

8. _____ the buttons for plane schedules.

9. _____ to the time and temperature.

10. _____ to put up Raquel's bookshelves.

D. Questions and Yes/No Answers

Ming **wanted** to go to Hong Kong.

Did Ming **want** to go to Hong Kong?

Circle the correct short answer for the questions.

1. Did Ming want to go to Hong Kong for the wedding?

Yes, she did.   No, she didn't.

2. Did Raquel find a cheap ticket to Hong Kong?

Yes, she did.   No, she didn't.

3. Did Ming want to buy the ticket for $899?

Yes, she did.   No, she didn't.

4. Did she call for a cheaper ticket?

Yes, she did.   No, she didn't.

5. Did she find a cheaper ticket?

Yes, she did.   No, she didn't

6. Did Sasha's friends call him from Russia?

Yes, they did.   No, they didn't.

7. Did Sasha call for bus schedules to the airport?

Yes, he did.   No, he didn't.

8. Did he find out the price of a plane ticket?

Yes, he did.   No, he didn't.

9. Did Raquel call Simon at work?

Yes, she did.   No, she didn't.

10. Did she talk to him?

Yes, she did.   No, she didn't.

E. Verbs: Simple Past—Irregular

come	came	have	had
cost	cost	leave	left
feel	felt	meet	met
fly	flew	take	took
get	got	tell	told
go	went	think	thought

To be: am/is → was; are → were.

Write verbs in the past tense in the sentences.

1. Ming and Sasha ——— **met** ——— at the International Center. (meet)

2. Sasha's friends ——————— from Russia. (fly)

3. Raquel ——————— to Ming's apartment. (come)

4. Simon ——————— a good time at the party. (have)

5. Ms. Lee ——————— Jorge and Elena about bank services. (tell)

6. A ticket to Hong Kong ——————— a lot of money. (cost)

7. Ming and Sasha ——————— on the city tour. (go)

8. Raquel ——————— the center at 8:00 P.M. (leave)

9. Jorge and Elena ——————— a nice apartment. (get)

10. Sasha ——————— the train to the airport. (take)

11. Raquel ——————— better after shopping. (feel)

12. Ming ——————— about her sister's wedding. (think)

F. Question Words

How **did** Simon and Raquel **meet**?

—They **met** on vacation.

Circle the correct question word.

1. (Where)/ When did Simon go? —To the Dominican Republic.
2. Who / How did he get there? —He flew.
3. When / How long was he there? —For one week.
4. Where / When did he meet Raquel? —At the hotel.
5. How / Why was she at the hotel? —She was on vacation.
6. Where / How did he invite her? —To dinner.
7. When / Where was the restaurant? —By the sea.
8. Who / What did they do after dinner? —They danced.
9. What / How did Simon ask Raquel to do? —To write to him.
10. How / When did Raquel feel when Simon left? —She felt sad.

G. Verbs in Questions

Write verbs in the past tense in the questions.

1. Where ___did___ Simon ___fly___ ? (fly)
2. Why _____ he _____ there? (go)
3. How _____ he _____ Raquel? (meet)
4. Why _____ she at the hotel? (be)
5. What _____ she _____ of Simon? (think)
6. How _____ the dinner? (be)
7. Why _____ Simon _____ Raquel to write him? (want)
8. How _____ they _____ ? (feel)
9. Why _____ they sad when the vacation ended? (be)
10. When _____ they _____ married? (get)

H. How much?/How long?

Draw a line to the correct answer.

1. How much is a cheap ticket to Hong Kong?
2. How long is the trip to the airport?
3. How much is a one-way train ticket to the airport?
4. How long was Simon in the Dominican Republic?
5. How much is a round-trip ticket to the airport?
6. How long will Raquel work at the center?
7. How much is an 800 phone call?
8. How long will Sasha wait at the airport?

a. $8.00.
b. Until 9:00 P.M.
c. $12.00.
d. Until late.
e. It's free.
f. Thirty minutes.
g. About $900.
h. One week.

I. Possessives: Nouns, Adjectives, and Pronouns

1. Raquel is __Simon's__ wife.
2. Elena is _____ wife.
3. Ming is _____ friend.
4. Simon is __Raquel's__ husband.
5. Jorge is _____ husband.
6. Sasha is _____ friend.

ADJECTIVE + NOUN	PRONOUN	ADJECTIVE + NOUN	PRONOUN
my ticket	mine	our house	ours
your phone	yours	your class	yours
his furniture	his		
her apartment	hers	their car	theirs
its food	—		

Cross out the possessive pronoun + noun and write the possessive adjective.

7. Where are the tickets?

   ~~My ticket~~ **Mine** is on the table and ~~your ticket~~ **your ticket** is on the desk.

8. Where are the phones?

   His phone is in his hand, and *her phone* is in her bag.

9. Where is the dog's food?

   Its food is on the floor.

10. Where is your house?

    Our house is near *your house*—on the same street.

11. Where are the cars?

    Their car is in the parking lot, and *our car* is on the street.

J. Modals: *Should, Could, Might*

Read the dialogues and answer the questions.

SASHA: Ming, what time **should** I go to the airport? (*advice*)

MING: What time will the plane arrive?

SASHA: It **should** arrive at 9:00 P.M. (*probability*), but it **could** be late. (*possibility*)

MING: It **might** be early, too. (*possibility*) Take the 8:00 train to be safe.

SASHA: That's a good idea.

1. What time **should** the plane arrive? —At ____**9:00 P.M.**____

2. What time **could** it arrive? —Before/after _____

3. Which train **should** Sasha take to the airport?

    —The _____ train.

MING: It takes a long time to go through immigration.

SASHA: I know. It **might** take half an hour.

MING: You **could** watch TV in the waiting area.

SASHA: I **should** bring a book to read.

MING: Yes, you **might** not get home until eleven.

4. How long **might** it take to pass through immigration and customs? — _____ minutes.

5. What time **could** Sasha's friends be ready to go?

    —After _____ .

6. What time **might** he get home? —Around _____ .

K. Real People...Real Language

1. Making a local directory assistance call...

Write the answers on the lines.

a. City: ____**Boston**____

b. Listing: **Boston Museum of Science**

c. Number: _____

2. Calling for the time and temperature...

Circle what you hear.

a. At the tone, the time will be   (3:35 pm)   3:15 pm

b. The temperature is: 73°   93°

3. Calling for the hours of the Science Museum...

Write what you hear.

a. open Tuesday through __**Sunday**__

b. hours are _____ A.M. to _____ P.M.

c. Admission: _____ adults, _____ students,

_____ children

4. Calling for plane fares...

Circle what you hear.

a. Hong Kong   (New York)

b. round trip   one-way

c. $19 $90

....

VIDEO TRANSCRIPT

Watch and Listen

Raquel: So, your sister's getting married.

Ming: Yes, I wish I could go to Hong Kong for the wedding.

Raquel: Well, some airlines have cheap flights to Hong Kong. You know what, we can look in the paper. Here's something right here: a round-trip ticket for $899.

Ming: Not bad, but I can't afford it.

Raquel: Let's call and see if there's anything cheaper.

Ming: Okay, what's the number?

Raquel: 1-800-555-TOUR.

Ming: Tour?

Raquel: Yes, you have to press the buttons for the letters.

Ming: Oh, I see... T-O-U-R... The line is busy.

Raquel: Well, that's okay. Let's try again later.

(doorbell sounds)

Ming: Come in. It's open.

Raquel: Who is that?

Ming: Sasha said he might stop by.

Sasha: Ming! ... Oh, hello, Raquel.

Raquel: Hi, Sasha.

Ming: Come in. Sit down.

Sasha: Guess what!

Raquel: What?

Sasha: An old friend from Russia called me. He and his family are arriving today!

Ming: Really?

Sasha: Yes, they finally got a visa after two years.

Ming: That's so exciting!

Sasha: I'm going to the airport to pick them up. Do you want to come?

Ming: Okay.

Raquel: How are you going to get there?

Sasha: By train. But I have to call for the times. They're arriving on a 9:00 flight.

Ming: You can use this phone.

Raquel: I think the number for the train schedules is 555-9244.

Sasha: The airport train, right?

Raquel: Right. It takes about half an hour.

TRAINCHECK: Welcome to TrainCheck. For city trains, press 1. For commuter trains, press 2. For city train routes, press 1. For schedules and prices, press 2. The A train, which goes to the airport, leaves every fifteen minutes from Central Station. It takes approximately 30 minutes. The fare is $8 one way, or $12 round trip.

Sasha: It costs only $12 for a round-trip ticket to the airport. Not bad.

Raquel: No, no bad at all.... I have to tell Simon I'm going to be working late today. Ming, can I borrow your phone?

Ming: Of course.

Raquel: Hi, may I speak to Simon, please?...Oh, that's right, he's still in class. Can I leave a message for him?...Yes, it's Raquel. Could you please tell him that I'm going to be working late tonight?...Thank you...Okay. Bye...So, Ming, are you all unpacked?

Ming: Yes, mostly. But I still have to put up bookshelves in my room.

Sasha: I can help you with that, Ming.

Ming: Oh, thank you. Let me show you how I want it set up.

Raquel: That's all for now. Here are a few phrases you can use on the phone.

To ask to speak to someone, you can say:

> **May I speak to** Simon, please?   or
>
> **Is** Sasha **there?**

To introduce yourself on the phone, you say:

> **Hi, this is** Raquel.   or
>
> **It's** Raquel.

To leave a message for someone, you can say:

> **Please call me back.**   or
>
> **I'll call you back later.**
>
> **My number is** 555-3890.   or
>
> **You can reach me at** 555-3890.

Now let's listen to people using different services on the phone.

Answer Key

Unit 1 At The International Center: Introductions

A. Introductions
1. Hello 2. are 3. Fine 4. you
5. This 6. meet 7. is 8. My

B. Countries
1. China 2. Russia 3. United States
4. Mexico

C. Professions
1. d. 2. a. 3. e. 4. c. 5. b.

D. Verbs: Present Tense—*To Be*
1. is 2. are 3. is 4. is 5. is 6. is
7. are 8. am 9. are 10. are

E. Contractions
1. you're 2. they're 3. it's 4. I'm
5. we're 6. he's

F. Negatives
1. am not 2. are not 3. is not 4. is not
5. is not 6. is not 7. are not
8. are not 9. are not 10. is not

G. Negative Contractions
1. he's not/he isn't 2. they're not/they
aren't 3. we're not/we aren't 4. I'm
not 5. you're not/you aren't 6. she's
not/she isn't

H. Questions and Yes/No Answers
1. No, he is not. 2. Yes, he is. 3. Yes,
she is. 4. No, I am not. 5. No, they
are not. 6. Is Simon from the United
States? 7. Are you from Hong Kong?
8. Are Sasha and Ming at the
International Center? 9. Are Elena and
Jorge hungry? 10. Is the food on the
table?

I. Question Words
1. Who 2. Who 3. What 4. Who
5. Where 6. What 7. Where 8. What

J. Short answers
1. Ming is. 2. From Mexico. 3. Sasha
is. 4. From the D.R. 5. Simon is.

K. Country/Nationality/Language
1. Portuguese 2. Dominican 3. China
4. —— 5. —— 6. —— 7. Mexican
8. Russian 9. American 10. ——

L. People/Countries
1. Dominican Republic 2. Chinese
3. Mexico 4. Russian 5. United States
6. Spanish 7. Russian 8. Chinese
9. English

M. Dialogue
1. Simon 2. you, is 3. meet 4. My
5. you 6. Nice 7. you 8. this 9. meet
10. pleasure 11. Are, I

N. Professions and Workplaces
1. teacher 2. cashier 3. waitress
4. engineer

O. Real People...Real Language
1. computer 2. student 3. Taiwan
4. consultant 5. Mexican 6. Ukraine
7. Taipei 8. Colombia 9. mother
10. Puerto Rico 11. Jamaica
12. technology

Unit 2 A City Tour: The Time and Date

A. Days, Months, and Seasons
1. Sunday, Monday, Tuesday, Wednesday, Thursday, Friday, Saturday 2. March, April, May 3. June, July, August 4. September, October, November 5. December, January, February

B. Verbs: Present Continuous—To Be + __ing
1. is waiting 2. is coming 3. are talking 4. is asking 5. is looking 6. is telling 7. is walking 8. are going
9. are writing 10. am finishing

C. Negatives
1. is not going 2. is not waiting 3. are not shopping 4. is not having 5. is not talking 6. are not sitting 7. am not getting 8. are not eating 9. are not watching 10. is not sleeping

D. Yes/No Answers
1. Yes, she is. 2. No, he isn't./No, he's not. 3. Yes, it is. 4. Yes, they are.
5. Yes, it is. 6. No, they aren't./No, they're not. 7. Yes, it is. 8. Yes, they are. 9. No, he isn't./No, he's not.
10. Yes it is.

E. Question Words
1. When 2. Which 3. When
4. Which 5. When 6. When
7. When 8. Which 9. When

F. Prepositions of Time
1. at, in 2. in 3. on 4. at 5. on 6. at, at 7. in 8. on 9. in 10. on

G. Dialogue
1. sorry 2. right 3. at 4. What
5. you 6. are 7. ——Let's 8. on
9. fall

H. Number Practice
(no answers)

I. Telling Time
1. 1:10/one-ten 2. 2:25/two-twenty-five 3. 12:15/twelve-fifteen
4. 8:55/eight-fifty-five 5. 11:45/eleven-forty-five 6. 9:05/nine-o-five
7. 3:35/three-thirty-five 8. 4:30/ four-thirty 9. 5:00/five o'clock
10. 7:20/seven-twenty 11. 6:50/six-fifty 12. 10:40/ten-forty

J. What's the date?
1. Thursday 2. Tuesday
3. Wednesday 4. Friday 5. Monday

K. Real People...Real Language
1. a. 8:30 b. 7:00 c. 8:00 d. 11:00
e. 7:00 f. 6:00 g. 9:00
2. a. dinner in a restaurant b. stopped having parties c. party with family and friends d. no party e. dinner and phone calls
3. a. summer b. winter c. summer
d. fall e. spring f. summer g. summer

Unit 3 Asking for Directions

A. What is it?
1. stop 2. box 3. post 4. movie

B. Odd One Out
1. letter 2. stamp 3. movie 4. theater

C. Opposites
1. right 2. off 3. far 4. there

D. Verbs: Simple Present
1. sits 2. answers 3. asks 4. wants
5. needs 6. takes 7. live 8. eat
9. speak 10. study

E. Negatives
1. doesn't speak 2. doesn't drive
3. doesn't work 4. don't go 5. doesn't
paint 6. don't know 7. don't drink
8. don't buy 9. doesn't drive 10. don't
watch 10. doesn't eat

F. Yes/No Answers
1. Yes, he does. 2. No, they don't.
3. Yes, I do. 4. No, she doesn't.
5. No, you don't. 6. Yes, it does.
7. Yes, he does. 8. Yes, I do. 9. No,
they don't. 10. Yes, you do.

G. Short Answers
1. Elena does. 2. Near the
supermarket. 3. Jorge does. 4. Two
blocks. 5. Raquel does. 6. I do. 7. It
costs $1.50. 8. Four stops. 9. Near
the pharmacy. 10. Ming does.

H. Questions
1. Where 2. Where 3. Who 4. How
much 5. Who 6. How many 7. How
much 8. Who 9. How many
10. Where

I. Plurals
1. banks 2. blocks 3. letters 4. maps
5. stops 6. trains

J. There is.../There are...
1. There are 2. There is 3. There is
4. There are 5. There are 6. There is

K. Prepositions of Place: In/On/At
1. in 2. at 3. on 4. at 5. at or in 6. in
7. on 8. on 9. at 10. on

L. Dialogue
1. post 2. bus 3. Where 4. Center
5. I'm 6. supermarket 7. you 8. are
9. am, go——

M. Real People...Real Language
1. a. 10, 5 b. —— c. 8 d. 10
2. a. 5 or 3 b. 2 c. 1 d. —— e. 1
3. a. walk b. drive c. drive d. drive
e. walk f. drive g. drive h. walk

Unit 4 Shopping For Food

A. Odd One Out
1. bananas 2. carrots 3. soup 4. juice
5. sauce

B. What is it?
1. apples, oranges, bananas,
strawberries 2. potatoes, onions,
carrots, tomatoes 3. milk, eggs, butter
4. soup, sauce

C. Verbs: Future with *Going To*
1. are going to go 2. is going to buy
3. is going to get 4. is going to look
for 5. are going to have 6. am going
to see 7. are going to drive 8. is going
to snow 9. are going to take 10. is
going to rent

D. Negatives

1. They aren't going to/They're not going to 2. She isn't going to/She's not going to 3. She isn't going to/She's not going to 4. She isn't going to/She's not going to 5. They aren't going to/They're not going to 6. He isn't going to/He's not going to 7. You aren't going to/You're not going to 8. I'm not going to 9. It isn't going to/It's not going to 10. We aren't going to/We're not going to

E. Yes/No Answers

1. No, she isn't. 2. Yes, she is. 3. No, she isn't 4. Yes, they are. 5. No, he isn't 6. No, they aren't.

F. Short Answers

1. d. 2. h. 3. i. 4. e. 5. a. 6. j. 7. b. 8. c. 9. g. 10. f.

G. Questions

1. How much 2. How many 3. How much 4. How many 5. How many 6. How much 7. How many 8. How many 9. How much 10. How much

H. Singular/Plural Nouns

1. apples 2. bananas 3. carrots 4. eggs 5. onions 6. potatoes 7. tomatoes 8. strawberries 9. raspberries 10. cherries

I. Money

Raquel: Total = $9.54 Change = $.46
Ming: Total = $6.36 Change = $3.64
Elena: Total = $9.21 Change = $.79

J. Count and Noncount Nouns

1. apples, potatoes, eggs, bananas, onions, oranges, tomatoes 2. bread, soup, juice, rice, milk, spaghetti, tomato sauce

K. Recipe: Jorge's Tacos

BEEF, LETTUCE TOMATO, SALT, TACO, CHEESE, CREAM, SALSA

L. Dialogue

1. you 2. cook 3. What 4. tacos 5. need 6. cheese 7. do 8. some 9. tonight 10. need 11. dinner 12. her

M. Containers

Other answers are also correct!
1. apples, grapefruit 2. beer, champagne 3. pasta, rice 4. plantains, collard greens 5. peaches, tuna 6. soy milk, eggs 7. cauliflower, 8. mayonnaise, kimchee 9. cookie dough 10. ointment, hand cream

N. Real People...Real Language

1.a. once a month b. once or twice a week c. hardly ever d. once every two weeks 2.a. cheese b. eggs c. rice 3.a. onions b. bananas c. rice d. sauce 4.a. 2 b. 2 c. 2 5. a. $80 to $100 b. $50 c. $150 d. $200

Unit 5: Finding an Apartment

A. Odd One Out

1. bed 2. shower 3. oven 4. microwave

B. Verbs: Present Tense—Can/Can't

1. can 2. can't 3. can 4. can't 5. can't 6. can 7. Can/No, he can't. 8. Can/Yes, he can. 9. Can/Yes, she can. 10. Can/No, she can't.

C. Verbs: Past Tense—Could/Couldn't

1. could 2. couldn't 3. could 4. couldn't 5. could 6. could 7. Could/No, they couldn't. 8. Could/Yes, they could 9. Could/Yes, he could. 10. Could/No, she couldn't.

D. *Can/Can't or Could/Couldn't*
1. can't 2. could 3. could 4. can't
5. couldn't 6. can 7. couldn't
8. could

E. Short Answers
1. Yes, I can. 2. No, he couldn't.
3. Yes, they can. 4. Yes, she could.
5. Yes, I can. 6. No, he couldn't.
7. Yes, we can. 8. No, I couldn't.
9. No, they can't. 10. Yes, she could.

F. Adjectives: Opposites
1. new, large, expensive 2. old, small,
pretty 3. large, old, interesting

G. Adjectives: Comparative and Superlative
1. large, larger, largest 2. small,
smaller, smallest 3. new, newer,
newest 4. old, older, oldest 5. heavy,
heavier, heaviest 6. pretty, prettier,
prettiest 7. easy, easier, easiest
8. expensive, more expensive, most
expensive 9. interesting, more
interesting, most interesting
10. difficult, less difficult, least difficult
11. Serious, less serious, least serious

H. More Comparatives and Superlatives
1. older 2. newer 3. larger 4. more
expensive 5. more interesting 6. more
modern 7. newest 8. cheapest 9. most
expensive 10. most interesting

I. Questions: Which/Which One
1. Which 2. Which one 3. Which
4. Which one 5. Which 6. Which one
7. Which one 8. Which 9. Which one
10. Which one

J. Dialogue
1. nice 2. Where 3. near 4. much
5. expensive 6. many 7. large 8. can
9. you 10. tomorrow 11. like
12. can't

K. Newspapers: Classified Ads
Apt. 1: 1, 1, yes, yes, yes, $800 Apt. 2:
3, 1 1/2, no, no, yes, $1,500 Apt. 3: 2,
2, yes, yes, yes, $1,200 Apt. 4: 4, 2,
yes, yes, yes, $2,000

L. Real People...Real Language
1.a. Mission Hill b. Hyde Park
c. West Roxbury d. North Cambridge
2.a. realtor b. friend c. doctor
d. driving e. real estate agent 3.a. 2 b.
3 c. 3 d. 3 e. 2 4.a. $575 b. $300
each/$600 total c. $2,500 before/
$1,500 now d. high e. $800 5.a. yes
b. no c. yes d. no e. no

Unit 6: Opening a Bank Account

A. Vocabulary Practice
1. savings account, to save money
2. ATM card, credit card 3. checking
account, paycheck, traveler's checks 4.
deposit 5. withdraw 6. teller
7. cash

B. Verbs: Future with *Will/Won't*
1. will 2. won't 3. will 4. will 5. will
6. won't 7. will 8. will 9. won't
10. will

C. Yes/No Answers
1. No, they won't. 2. Yes, they will.
3. Yes, they will. 4. Yes, they will.
5. No, they won't. 6. Yes, I will.
7. No, it won't. 8. Yes, we will.
9. Yes, it will. 10. No, I won't.

D. Questions
1. h. 2. a. 3. b. 4. c. 5. f. 6. g. 7. d.
8. i. 9. j. 10. e.

E. Questions: How often?
1. How often 2. How often 3. How
often 4. How often 5. How often
6. How often 7. How often 8. How
often

F. Adverbs of Frequency
1. always 2. usually 3. always
4. sometimes 5. always 6. never
7. rarely 8. often 9. usually 10.
always

G. *Too* and *Enough*
1. too 2. enough 3. too 4. enough
5. too 6. enough 7. too 8. too
9. enough 10. enough

H. Object Pronouns
1. Simon will meet her at the center.
2. Jorge and Elena will ask him to
paint their new apartment. 3. The
bank teller will mail it. 4. Ming will
serve them in the restaurant. 5. Raquel
will take it to the library. 6. Simon
gives them homework. 7. You can get
it from the ATM. 8. Jorge can teach
him to cook. 9. Elena can show her
her new apartment. 10. Sasha can take
it to work.

I. If Clauses: Bank Advice
1. application 2. joint 3. balance
4. balance 5. ATM 6. savings account
7. credit 8. checks 9. loan 10. interest

J. A Bank Statement
1. $850 2. 11-01 3. $68.12 4. 2
5. $1,372.84

K. Conjunctions: *And* Versus *Or*
1. and 2. or/and 3. or 4. and 5. and
6. and/or

L. Conjunctions: *And* Versus *But*
1. but 2. and 3. but not 4. and
5. but 6. but not

M. Real People...Real Language
1.a. BankBoston b. BankBoston
c. Fleet Bank d. BankBoston e. U.S.
Trust 2.a. big banks b. big
c. small d. big e. small f. big g. big
3.a. checking/savings b. checking/
savings/ATM c. checking/savings/
ATM d. ATM a lot e. 3 or 4 times a
week 4. a. twice a week b. not often
c. twice a week d. Checks or credit
cards
5.a. credit cards b. checks c. checks
d. credit cards e. credit cards f. checks
g. credit cards h. checks

Unit 7: Using the Telephone

A. Vocabulary Practice
1. pick 2. hang 3. message 4. rings 5.
operator 6. phone card 7. toll-free 8.
flight 9. schedule 10. one-way

B. Verbs: Simple Past—Regular
1. wanted 2. looked 3. dialed
4. asked 5. called 6. received
7. picked 8. pressed 9. listened
10. offered 1. wanted 2. loocked 3.
dialed 4. asked 5. called
6. received 7. picked 8. pressed 9.
listened 10. offered

C. Negatives
1. She didn't want 2. She didn't look
3. She didn't dial 4. She didn't ask
5. They didn't call 6. They didn't
receive 7. He didn't pick 8. He didn't

press 9. He didn't listen 10. He didn't offer

D. Questions and Yes/No Answers
1. Yes, she did. 2. Yes, she did. 3. No, she didn't. 4. Yes, she did. 5. No, she didn't 6. Yes, they did. 7. Yes, he did. 8. No, he didn't. 9. Yes, she did. 10. No, she didn't.

E. Verbs: Simple Past—Irregular
1. met 2. flew 3. came 4. had 5. told 6. cost 7. went 8. left 9. got 10. took 11. felt 12. thought

F. Question Words
1. Where 2. How 3. How long 4. Where 5. Why 6. Where 7. Where 8. What 9. What 10. How

G. Verbs in Questions
1. did, fly 2. did, go 3. did, meet 4. was 5. did, think 6. was 7. did, want 8. did, feel 9. were 10. did, get

H. How much?/How long?
1. g. 2. f 3. a. 4. h. 5. c. 6. d. 7. e. 8. b.

I. Possessives: Nouns, Adjectives, and Pronouns
1. Simon's 2. Jorge's 3. Sasha's 4. Raquel's 5. Elena's 6. Ming's 7. Mine, yours 8. His, hers 9. —— 10. Ours, yours 11. Theirs, ours

J. Modals: *Should, Could, Might*
1. 9:00 2. 9:00 3. 8:00 4. 30 5. 10:00 6. 11:00

K. Real People...Real Language
1.a. Boston, b. Boston Museum of Science c. 555-1700 2.a. 3:35, b. 73° 3.a. Sunday, b. 10, G, c. $10, $8, $6 4.a. New York, b. round trip, c. $90

Word List

a few
a little
a lot
account
afternoon
again
agent
aisle
always
American
and
answering
    machine
any
apartment
apples
are
area code
ATM
bag
balance
bananas
bank
basket
bathroom
bedroom
birthday
block
bottle
box
Brazil
Brazilian
bread
building

bunch
bus
bus stop
busy signal
butter
bye
call
can
cardinal numbers
cards
carrots
cart
carton
cash
cashier
center
chair
cheap
check
child
children
China
Chinese
classified ads
clothing store
collector
college
Colombia
Colombian
Colorado
community
company
computer
consultant

container
convenience
corner
could
cross the street
dark
date
daughter
day
deposit
dial
dining room
directory
    assistance
do
does
doesn't
Dominican
Dominican
    Republic
don't
electricity
Elena
engineer
evening
expensive
father
fee
fine
floor
French
gas
Georgia
get off

get on
go straight
good morning
good-bye
great
had
Haiti
Haitian
half-past
hang up
has
has to
have
have to
he
hello
her
hers
hi
high
his
home
Hong Kong
house
how
how long
how many
how much
how often
hungry
husband
I
identification
information

interest
international
is
it
its
Jamaica
Jamaican
Japan
Japanese
jar
Jorge
juice
know
Korea
Korean
large
later
laundry
lease
leave
letter
light
living room
loaf
loan
local
long distance
low
machine
mailbox
math
mechanic
meet
message
Mexican
Mexico
milk
mine
Ming
minimum
modern
months
Moscow
mother

movie theater
my
nationalities
negative
neighborhood
never
new
New York
newspaper
nice
night
o'clock
office
often
old-fashioned
onions
operator
oranges
ordinal numbers
our
ours
painter
parking
people
pharmacy
phrases
pick up
Port-au-Prince
Portugal
Portuguese
post office
potatoes
pound
Puerto Rico
Puerto Rican
quarter
Raquel
rarely
real estate
restaurant
rice
ring
Russia
Russian

Sasha
sauce
school
secretary
see
seldom
service
she
should
signature
Simon
small
social worker
some
sometimes
son
soon
soup
Spain
Spanish
stamp
statement
stick
store
strawberries
student
subway
supermarket
table
tai-chi
Taipei
Taiwan
teacher
technology
telephone
teller
Thailand
that
their
theirs
they
this
time
to

today
token
tomatoes
tomorrow
train
traveler's checks
turn left
turn right
Ukraine
United States
Uruguay
usually
utilities
vacation
verb
very well
Vietnam
Vietnamese
waitress
we
where
wife
will
window
withdraw
word
would
wrong number
years
yogurt
you
your
yours

NOTES

NOTES